T0360749

Cambridge Elements ☰

Elements in Chinese Economy and Governance
edited by
Luke Qi Zhang
Fudan University
Mingxing Liu
Peking University
Daniel Mattingly
Yale University

MERITOCRACY OR PATRONAGE?

Political Foundations of China's Economic Transition

Fubing Su
Vassar College

Ran Tao
The Chinese University of Hong Kong

CAMBRIDGE
UNIVERSITY PRESS

Shaftesbury Road, Cambridge CB2 8EA, United Kingdom

One Liberty Plaza, 20th Floor, New York, NY 10006, USA

477 Williamstown Road, Port Melbourne, VIC 3207, Australia

314–321, 3rd Floor, Plot 3, Splendor Forum, Jasola District Centre, New Delhi – 110025, India

103 Penang Road, #05–06/07, Visioncrest Commercial, Singapore 238467

Cambridge University Press is part of Cambridge University Press & Assessment, a department of the University of Cambridge.

We share the University's mission to contribute to society through the pursuit of education, learning and research at the highest international levels of excellence.

www.cambridge.org
Information on this title: www.cambridge.org/9781009507974

DOI: 10.1017/9781009507967

First published 2024

A catalogue record for this publication is available from the British Library.

ISBN 978-1-009-50797-4 Hardback
ISBN 978-1-009-50800-1 Paperback
ISSN 2976-5625 (online)
ISSN 2976-5617 (print)

Meritocracy or Patronage?

Political Foundations of China's Economic Transition

Elements in Chinese Economy and Governance

DOI: 10.1017/9781009507967
First published online: November 2024

Fubing Su
Vassar College

Ran Tao
The Chinese University of Hong Kong

Author for correspondence: Fubing Su, fusu@vassar.edu

Abstract: This Element interrogates the theoretical and empirical validities of two dominant theories about the Chinese state in the post-Mao period. The authors argue that the meritocratic view has under-theorized the innate contradiction between officials' personal competence and their political loyalty. In order to survive political struggles, political leaders need to rely on patronage networks to recruit followers and solidify trust, often at the expense of official competence. The popular view also misrepresents China's cadre assessment system in several important ways. The authors supplement this theoretical and anecdotal evidence with a systematic study of provincial-level officials between 1978 and 2020. Contrary to the meritocratic view, leaders' economic performance does not increase their promotion chances. Work ties with central leaders, on the other hand, have provided provincial officials with advantage in promotion. This Element contributes to general theories of the autocratic state and informs the debate about autocratic growth in the political economy literature.

Keywords: meritocracy, patronage, China, development, political economy

ISBNs: 9781009507974 (HB), 9781009508001 (PB), 9781009507967 (OC)
ISSNs: 2976-5625 (online), 2976-5617 (print)

Contents

1 Introduction

The way a state is governed in a country has far-reaching consequences that extend well beyond the realm of politics. It not only determines the level of political freedom citizens can enjoy but also profoundly influences the quality of life, economic potential, and overall societal development. In his groundbreaking work, North (1981) emphasizes the critical role of secure property rights in the ascent of the European economy in modern times. An even more profound insight is North's reminder to all researchers that, although property rights are crucial, a theory of the state must be incorporated to comprehend why advantageous property rights arrangements were not adopted in some countries in the first place. This should be a primary inquiry for political economists seeking to explain the complexities of economic development and underdevelopment throughout world history.

This insight has served as a major inspiration for generations of scholars, propelling them to investigate the political underpinnings of economic development. When explaining cross-country differences in economic development, the type of government in place emerges as a central point of contention among political economists. Many researchers in this field hold the view that democratic forms of government offer significant promise. North and Weingast (1989) assert that while a strong state is a prerequisite for safeguarding property rights, it is the checks and balances inherent in democratic governments that possess the institutional capacity to prevent state predation and guarantee the security of property rights. A case in point is the Glorious Revolution of 1688, which, through the establishment of parliamentary supremacy, allowed the British monarch to instill confidence in creditors and lay a robust foundation for the Industrial Revolution. Looking at it from a different angle, Bhagwati (2002) contends that the advantages of a democratic regime go beyond the mechanism of property rights. They extend to its ability to maintain peace on both domestic and international fronts and avoid costly policy errors by tapping into the wealth of information from all strata of society. Acemoglu and Robinson (2020) expand upon these concepts and further suggest that democratic regimes provide political openness that nurtures a climate of market competition, and harness the immense pool of human potential for driving technological advancements. These elements serve as the bedrock for fostering sustainable economic growth in the long run.

In contrast, autocratic regimes tend to concentrate power in the hands of a select few, thereby limiting the political freedoms of the vast majority. The unequal distribution of resources and opportunities limit the broader societal and economic development. Property rights are frequently violated by an arbitrary state, eroding business confidence in making productive invest-ments (Przeworski and Limongi 1993). While individuals in close proximity to the ruling authority may enjoy more secure property rights, their numbers are insufficient to uplift the entire economy. These same individuals also benefit from privileged market access and maintain monopolistic control in various industries. The failure to educate and involve the majority of the general population means that the country cannot fully harness the collective potential of its people and thus impedes the development of a more inclusive and equitable society (Acemoglu and Robinson 2012; De Mesquita and Smith 2011).

An emerging and increasingly relevant field of inquiry has attempted to establish democratic advantages that extend beyond these structural elements of democratic governance and delves into the personal qualities of its leaders. Competitive elections provide citizens with an explicit mechanism to evaluate their leaders' performance in relation to that of their predecessors and neighbor-ing counterparts. Observing the relative successes and failures of their leaders, citizens are more likely to be more discerning in their choices and elect candidates with proven track records of competence and ethical conduct (Besley and Case 1992; Cooter 2003). This selection process not only acts as a filter to screen out low-quality individuals but also incentivizes political leaders to make enlight-ened policy decisions and deliver superior economic outcomes for the constitu-ents (Besley, Montalvo, and Reynal-Querol 2011; Jones and Olken 2005). Conversely, autocratic systems often exhibit a concentration of power that is conducive to nepotism and cronyism. In such environments, the selection of leaders is frequently based on factors other than merit and competence. Leaders appoint relatives and close associates to key positions of authority, regardless of their ability to govern effectively. This nepotistic approach hinders the overall competence level of autocratic governments and weakens the quality of policy-making and economic outcomes within those jurisdictions (Acemoglu, Egorov, and Sonin 2012). The lack of competitive elections and accountability mechan-isms in these systems also perpetuates suboptimal leadership. These leaders often prioritize their own interests or those of a small elite, leading to policy decisions that do not align with the broader welfare of the population (Besley and Reynal-Querol 2011; Dal Bó et al. 2017).

In recent years, a growing body of academic work has begun to challenge these conventional thoughts surrounding the advantages of democratic govern-ance. The claim that competitive elections consistently select competent lead-ers, in particular, is now under scrutiny. Some argue that the fierce competition in elections can inadvertently thrust populist figures into leadership positions, with their emphasis on popularity often overshadowing considerations of competence (Buckley and Reuter 2019). The recent electoral successes of various populist leaders worldwide, representing a broad ideological spectrum from left-wing to right-wing and nationalist positions, further reinforce this skeptical perspective. These occurrences have become so commonplace that it prompts a reasonable question: could this phenomenon be inherent to the democratic system itself? Figures like Donald Trump in the United States, Rodrigo Duterte in the Philippines, Viktor Orbán in Hungary, Andrés Manuel López Obrador in Mexico, and Evo Morales in Bolivia have all ascended to power. Their leadership has been marked by contentious policies and questionable economic and social outcomes, adding weight to the argument that electoral competition may not always guarantee competent leadership.

The rapid ascent of the Chinese economy over the past four decades presents a compelling contrast. Since the late 1970s, China has undergone an extraordinary economic transformation, propelling itself to be ranked one of the world's largest and fastest-growing economies. With an impressive average annual gross domestic product (GDP) growth rate of 9.5 percent between 1979 and 2019, China's economic boom has lifted hundreds of millions of people out of poverty, establishing it as the second-largest economy globally (Brandt and Rawski 2020; Naughton 2006). While market reforms in China's rural, urban, and international economies have played a pivotal role in this success, political economists widely recognize the significant influence of certain qualities inherent in the Chinese state, partially stemming from its highly autocratic rule by the Communist Party. Specifically, China's centralized cadre management system has facilitated the recruitment of highly talented individuals into leadership positions, contributing to the nation's remarkable economic achievements (Blanchard and Shleifer 2001; Maskin, Qian, and Xu 2000). This counternarrative suggests that autocratic systems, when structured around meritocratic principles, can achieve significant developmental outcomes. Bell (2016) posits that this model presents a viable alternative to the democratic development model in the West, potentially offering superior outcomes. The ongoing debate surrounding these issues holds profound implications for our comprehension of good governance and development within the global context. For many impoverished nations governed by autocratic regimes, the Chinese model offers an alternative to the traditional democratic development path. We intend to contribute to this high-stakes deliberation by scrutinizing the Chinese case, often held up as a prime example within the dissenting camp. Specifically, we inquire if the Chinese state has operated as meritocratically as its proponents assert.

To effectively address this question, it is imperative to delve into the intricacies of state-building in China. After an extensive survey of the existing literature on this subject, encompassing both theoretical and empirical works, we distill two prominent theories that have significantly influenced scholars' perspectives in Section 2. One prevailing argument posits that China remains entrenched in informal policies reminiscent of the Mao era. This perspective asserts that power is personal and patronage constitutes the fundamental organizational principle in governing personnel appointments in the party-state. Leaders reward unwavering loyalty with key party and government positions. In return, these trusted clients and followers offer valuable resources and political supports, aiding leaders in their competitions and ensuring political survival amid internal power struggles. Numerous studies, both anecdotal and systematic, affirm the prevalence of factionalism in China. Conversely, another school of thought contends that post-Mao China has undergone significant transformations aimed at reestablishing state legitimacy through rational governance and economic development. Central to this argument is a national cadre assessment system that quantitatively evaluates leaders' performance across a list of tasks at various levels of government. Individuals with exceptional capabilities for driving economic growth have risen through tournament-like competitions. This constitutes the formal and institutionalized foundation of China's meritocratic state.

The idea of officials striving for promotion based on meritocratic principles holds an appealing theoretical promise, especially for Chinese political economists frustrated by the messiness of autocratic politics. This notion has gained traction among young researchers who lean on this assumption to construct increasingly sophisticated models explaining politics and economy in China. In Section 3, we highlight three fundamental issues with this meritocratic perspective. Primarily, applying a bureaucratic model to local leaders risks blurring the important distinction between bureaucrats and politicians. This shortcut overlooks the perpetual struggle for survival that politicians face within an autocratic state. When power takes center stage in intellectual discussions, it becomes evident that autocratic rulers tend to shun competent leaders. Therefore, competence and autocracy fundamentally clash. While some supporters of the meritocratic view argue that a common crisis among ruling elites could push them to prioritize fostering a Weberian state that values individual merit and achievements, this perspective disregards the fact that the purported economic crisis post-Mao's death was largely fabricated by Deng to undermine Mao's loyalists. Recent studies offer substantial evidence to refute this political myth. Furthermore, economic reforms inherently introduce uncertainty and resource redistribution, disrupting the existing political balance within the state. Post-Mao Chinese leaders were far from unified in their objectives and policies. Intense power struggles among prominent figures such as Deng Xiaoping, Hua Guofeng, Chen Yun, Zhao Ziyang, Li Peng, Jiang Zemin, Hu

Jintao, and Xi Jinping significantly shaped the ideological landscape surrounding reform agendas in their respective eras, leading to the ascent and decline of different factions. This disunity was not due to a lack of desire to foster economic growth; rather, it stemmed from their support for alternative policies that favored their political survival.

Secondly, the meritocratic view has misconstrued China's cadre assessment system in several crucial ways. Proponents suggest that central leaders have adopted a scoring system to assess all cadres' performance. They propose that numerical weights are assigned to all government and party tasks, especially emphasizing economic development tasks. This makes it possible to evaluate local cadres objectively and scientifically, hence a merit-based state. However, the actual cadre assessment system evaluates cadres' performance across multiple dimensions, with work achievement being just one of five aspects, and economic growth indicators holding even less significance in the total scores. Rather than relying on objective statistics, cadres' final merit ratings hinge on subjective evaluations by peers, subordinates, and superiors. Furthermore, there is no formal link between cadre merit ratings and promotions. The Central Committee of the Chinese Communist Party (CCP) and the Department of Organization treat cadre assessment and promotion as separate procedures, each with different regulatory rules. Instead of identifying capable individuals as the meritocratic view contends, the cadre assessment system is designed to compel the unwieldy cadre system to fulfill its basic functions at the grassroots level. The supposedly "objective" statistics are easily manipulated locally, rendering the assessment results practically unusable. Lastly, the notion of a highly centralized and uniform cadre management system is a misrepresentation of the reality. The Chinese cadre system is quite decentralized, with each tier responsible for assessing cadres one level below in the hierarchy. Consequently, cadre assessment exhibits significant variations concerning geographic location, administrative ranks, and development status. For practical purposes, it started to emerge in the second half of the 1990s, so using it to explain China's rapid economic growth in earlier decades does not align with reality.

The third critique concerns methodological inadequacies in existing empirical studies. While numerous studies explore cadre promotions and GDP growth, some positive findings stem from data errors and incorrect model specifications. For example, one of the most cited findings by Li and Zhou (2005) could not be replicated by Tao et al. (2010) after fixing some data errors. Wiebe (2024) has failed to replicate some research findings once some model misspecifications were corrected. Contradictory results also emerge regarding the effects on party and government leaders – some affirm meritocratic promotion for party secretaries only (Choi 2012), while others claim that it applies solely to government leaders like governors and mayors (Chen and Kung 2019). Still, some findings suggest uniform treatment of both party and government leaders within the meritocratic system (Landry, Lü, and Duan 2018; Zeng and Wong 2021). This inconsistency might relate to varied data ranges or administrative ranks. From a methodological perspective, however, existing studies tend to fall short in two aspects. Some empirical studies do not include patronage variables in their tests of the meritocratic hypothesis. Since these ties significantly influence both economic performance and career advancements simultaneously, models without these variables could potentially bias their conclusions. A more problematic issue is their inability to tackle latent variables. Failing to account for unobservable innate leader qualities in regressions skews their coefficient estimation of the economic growth variable. We discuss these issues in great details and propose to address these inadequacies by including individual leader fixed effects in our models. We exploit the exogenous change of top leadership to generate patronage tie switches, aiming for a more robust empirical basis in the theoretical debate.

To substantiate our theoretical, factual, and methodological critiques, we turn to systematic data and empirically study the elite mobility of Chinese provincial leaders in Section 4. These individuals occupy critical positions in China's political hierarchy, and their advancement often serves as a gateway to the country's most powerful governing circles. Upon scrutinizing the promotion patterns of these officials, we have discovered no corroborating evidence to support the assertion that individual merit has played a significant role in the central government's personnel decisions. This holds true consistently across various time periods marked by different core leaderships over the course of the past four decades. There are no exceptions, whether we examine high-growth periods, such as the early 1980s and the mid-1990s to mid-2000s, or low-growth phases, such as the late 1980s to the mid-1990s and the period from the 2010s to the present.

Regarding the alternative perspective of patronage politics, our results provide supportive evidence but do not precisely replicate previous findings. Researchers have identified various foundations for patronage ties in Chinese elite politics, including factors such as birthplace, college, affiliations with the Chinese Communist Youth League (CCYL), and princeling status. In our findings, we have observed that only relationships nurtured through close working associations with powerful patrons, especially the four core leaders: Deng Xiaoping, Jiang Zemin, Hu Jintao, and Xi Jinping, confer substantial and enduring advantages upon provincial officials in the high-stakes arena of personnel decisions. This finding remains robust even when we expand our definition of the top leadership to include General Party Secretaries and other

Political Bureau Standing Committee members, and apply more stringent promotion criteria while excluding positions in the National People's Congress and the National People's Political Consultative Conference.

This Element aims to make contributions to several important debates in the field of China studies and the broad field of political economy of development. It proposes a methodological remedy to the inference problem in studying Chinese official mobility. Numerous empirical tests have been carried out to verify these theories about Chinese state-building, but a consensus seems elusive as of now. Some studies have confirmed one side of the debate while rejecting the alternative: meritocratic promotion (Li and Zhou 2005; Zeng and Wong 2021) or factional selection (Opper, Nee, and Brehm 2015; Shih, Adolph, and Liu 2012). Still some results support both meritocracy and factionalism simultaneously (Chen and Kung 2016, 2019; Choi 2012; Jia, Kudamatsu, and Seim 2015; Landry, Lü, and Duan 2018). These bewildering findings partly reflect the fact that scholars have chosen to study different facets of the Chinese state or selected only certain time periods in their regression analyses. Some inconsistency also stems from data errors and model misspecifications (Fisman et al. 2020; Tao et al. 2010; Wiebe 2024). In our view, the failure to adequately deal with officials' unobserved personal traits in regression analyses is another underlying cause of these contradictory findings. Some innate traits, like cognitive ability, administrative aptitude, leadership style, interpersonal skills, personal values, and ambitions, can simultaneously decide provincial officials' economic performance, patronage ties, and career successes. Since these factors are unobservable, omitting them from regressions can bias the coefficients. We introduce individual fixed effects to estimate the within-individual effects. Essentially, we exploit the exogenous patronage tie switches caused by the leadership succession at the top of the hierarchy. The resulting coefficients capture the real impacts of patronage and performance, thereby situating the theoretical debate on a firmer empirical grounding than previous studies. Our comparative analysis shows that previous studies have significantly underestimated the impact of patronage ties. Implementing this strategy, however, requires long time series data that spans multiple generations of leaders to generate adequate switches. Our data includes all provincial leaders under multiple generations of ruling elites in post-Mao China, something infeasible for earlier researchers.

By demonstrating that the meritocracy argument lacks a solid empirical basis in China, we contribute to the theoretical development of autocracy. Because autocrats generally resist clear rules and formal institutions, autocratic governance has been typically conceptualized through a patronage model, with the usual traits of nepotism, corruption, and inefficiency. The proponents of the meritocratic view in recent years, as well as their predecessors in the developmental state tradition, have rightly acknowledged the imperative for rational governance in the age of modernization even for an autocratic state. But this mode of analysis has a tendency of reducing politics to simple administrative matters and under-theorizing power in autocracies. A model of autocratic governance must properly account for the autocrats' political logic when they contemplate the "Weberian" promotion rule. In a recent paper, some noted scholars in the field of public administration and bureaucracy urged fellow researchers to elevate politicians' survival instincts more explicitly in their analyses (Besley et al. 2021). In fact, this level of interrogation equally applies to those researchers who argue that both meritocracy and patronage have operated in concert inside the Chinese state. Loyalty is not an innate personal trait but rather a choice that clients make in high-stake power games. More competent people tend to attract bids from multiple patrons and are naturally less loyal (Egorov and Sonin 2011). These scholars have significantly under-theorized the trade-off between competence and loyalty. Studying the career path of Chinese military officials, Mattingly (2024) has shown some evidence supporting this trade-off view. Our study further demonstrates that this phenomenon is not limited to highly sensitive areas, like the military, but has permeated Chinese governance on a much broader scope.

Finally, our findings in this Element have important implications for the debate discussed at the outset: Does autocracy have any advantage in promoting meritocracy and high-quality growth? If Chinese leaders are not promoted on the basis of competence, the economic miracle during the reform cannot be explained by the high competence of its political leaders. Since China has been a poster child among dissenting groups, this calls into question the validity of the counterargument to the democratic advantage perspective in recent scholarly development. It should also discredit some attempts to embrace autocratic governance among development policy circles. However, our finding should not be interpreted as a rejection of the foundational belief of governance playing a significant role in economic development. Quite the contrary, our analysis points to two research directions that can advance this political-economic agenda. Scholars should examine the autocratic regime's advantage in mobilizing resources and suppressing societal resistance, which has played an essential role in molding China's particular growth model. Additionally, patronage politics can systematically shape economic policymaking, resource allocation, and the long-term trajectory of development. We will delve deeper into these topics in Section 5 and review recent publications along these lines of inquiry.

2 How Is the Chinese State Organized? Two Dominant Views

The Chinese state is characterized by a unique fusion of party and government apparatus, commonly referred to as the party-state system. At its core lies the Chinese Communist Party (CCP), which exercises paramount authority over all aspects of governance. The state institutions formally handle administrative functions, but the CCP permeates each cell of these institutions and supervises their adherence to the Party's ideologies and policies. Local authorities (province, prefecture/city, county, township) have gained significant autonomy over economic, social, and political management in post-Mao reforms, but as a unitary state, each tier is subordinate to the tier above it and, ultimately, all levels remain subordinate to the central party in Beijing. Within the CCP, leadership is hierarchical, with the final power vested in the Politburo Standing Committee (PSC), the apex decision-making body.

The CCP, like many autocratic regimes, places a strong emphasis on controlling its personnel and has established a highly centralized and complex system for managing its cadres. Institutionally, the Department of Organization oversees the operation of the nomenclature system and serves the party committees at each level of the hierarchy. Manion (2023) has summarized these formal rules and structures nicely in a volume on this topic. However, the core tenets guiding official qualifications have shifted back and forth between prioritizing "ideological purity" and "technical competence," in other words, valuing political loyalty versus professional expertise. During Mao's era, trust was placed in only a select few personal allies, and he was ruthless in suppressing political rivals and competing factions. However, in the period following Mao's death, there has been a push to place more importance on expertise when selecting government officials. Nevertheless, the effectiveness of this shift has been a subject of ongoing scholarly debate. In the extensive and continually expanding body of literature on this topic, two contrasting viewpoints have emerged.

2.1 Informal Power and Patronage Politics

Students of Chinese elite politics have long noted the prevalence of informal and personal power dynamics (Dittmer 1995; Nathan 1973). From grassroots levels to the highest echelons of power, patronage politics, and factional rivalry permeate the Chinese state. In many ways, this phenomenon is not surprising in the realm of politics. Across most human societies, people tend to associate with others who share commonalities like ethnicity, religion, values, and other traits (Lazarsfeld and Merton 1954). This innate human tendency assumes even greater significance in politics. Politicians in democracies often find it convenient and, at times, necessary to build powerful and loyal support bases through informal bonds and affinities, such as ethnicity, kinship, or alumni networks, in order to win elections and implement policies (Alesina, Baqir, and Easterly 1999; Cruz, Labonne, and Querubin 2017; De Mesquita et al. 2005). Autocracies, on the other hand, are even more susceptible to informal political dynamics. Unlike democracies, autocratic states lack credible rules and transparent environments that allow power contenders to openly disclose their ambitions, exhibit strength, observe their peers, and strike deals. Consequently, all essential political information-sharing and maneuvering occurs under the table (Shih 2008; Svolik 2012). This secrecy breeds systemic distrust among those holding power and between senior and junior officials inside an organization. Cultivating loyal followers not only enhances the political survival of senior officials themselves but also elevates their political weight in the eyes of their higher-ups.

Patronage relations established on the foundation of personal networks offer various mechanisms to cultivate and reinforce trust. At a fundamental level, personal ties, such as shared birthplaces, educational backgrounds, workplace associations, or affiliation with groups like the CCYL or involvement in the princeling circle (太子党) within the Chinese context, enable patrons to acquire valuable information about other aspiring political figures and select clients who share similar values and policy preferences (Kou 2014; Opper, Nee, and Brehm 2015). This alignment reduces the risk of betrayal in the future. Furthermore, patronage thrives on a specific exchange system where the patron's provision of protection, resources, and opportunities for career advancement is reciprocated by the client's valuable services. This mutual give-and-take between the "supportive exchange dyads" provides both parties with a strong incentive to maintain a trustworthy relationship (Landé 1973). In power struggles, where uncertainty and shifting alliances are commonplace, having reliable and steadfast partners becomes a strategic advantage. The more the patron and the client engage in a sustained, reciprocal exchange of resources and protection, the more they can count on each other when faced with challenges or opportunities.

However, given the private nature of these transactions, a long-term commitment may not always be sufficient to prevent defections. In such cases, personal networks serve as a semi-public platform for disciplining those who deviate from their commitments. When news of a defection spreads through these informal networks, other members of the same lineage, college friends, or former colleagues may cease cooperation with the patron or the client. More significantly, the stigma associated with defection can persist for an extended period, making it challenging for the individual to establish another patronage relationship in the future (Shih 2008). This network-based system plays a critical role in reinforcing trust and ensuring adherence to the terms of patronage.

Proponents of this perspective argue that Chinese elite politics revolves around factional maneuvering and patronage systems, which can be traced back to the CCP's founding years and Mao's rise to power (Huang 1994). In its formative phase, the CCP relied on "mountaintops" or base areas for its organizational strength and survival. Mao's strategic prowess allowed him to outmaneuver rival power contenders, securing the loyalty of both leaders and their respective power bases. This leadership style continued into the early years of the People's Republic of China, with Mao acknowledging that high-ranking cadres from his own "mountaintop," that is, the Fourth Red Army in the late 1920s and the First Front Army in the early 1930s, held more leadership positions than any other mountaintop in the Party (Guo 2001). Deng was equally masterful in leveraging patronage politics for political dominance. In fact, his own return to power after the arrest of the Gang of Four in October 1976 was bolstered by the persistent and collective lobbying from his former subordinates in the Second Field Army. This pressure from within the Party compelled the Central Committee under Hua Guofeng to reluctantly reinstate Deng, underscoring the significant value of patronage in political struggles. Once back in the power center, Deng reciprocated this loyalty by appointing numerous former subordinates from the 129th Division of the Eight Route Army, the Second Field Army, and the Southwest Military Region to key Party, government, and army positions. They played a pivotal role in the subsequent removal of Hua and his political allies from power (Guo 2001).

As one of the most important protégés of Deng, Zhao Ziyang also relied on personal networks to strengthen his political control. After he was promoted to the core leadership circle in 1978, Zhao brought in trusted subordinates, such as Tian Jiyun and Li Hao, from Sichuan and Guangdong provinces and strategically positioned them in important roles. However, he was not widely recognized for aggressively expanding his personal power networks. This approach may have been a strategic choice to allay any concerns Deng had about his political control. Given that Deng wielded informal authority and was watchful of any ambitious power contenders, even among his handpicked successors, Zhao's decision was likely aimed at maintaining Deng's trust. But this choice had its drawbacks, particularly during the critical moment of the 1989 student movement when Deng's backing for Zhao wavered. Regardless of Zhao's true intentions, his reluctance toward engaging in patronage politics was evidently not in line with the approaches of other leaders at that time. Even the 12th Central Committee of the CCP characterized the Party's cadre system in the 1980s using these terms:

> Some leading cadres do not adhere to the party's principles and violate organizational and personnel discipline. Some of them appoint or promote

individuals based on personal preferences, favoritism, or personal gain, or select people based on feudal clan and sectarian considerations. Others use various means to promote and appoint their children, relatives, or friends through 'backdoor' channels. Some offer positions in exchange for personal favors and engage in trading. Some disregard policy regulations to seek higher ranks and benefits for cadres within their own system and unit, leading to the upgrading of their affiliated units. Some comrades responsible for organizational and personnel work abandon their duties, act without principles, and even use their power for personal gain (Central Committee of the CCP 1986).

The Jiang Zemin and Hu Jintao eras were characterized by a degree of relative calm, compared with the often bloody and deadly factional infights under Mao and Deng. However, beneath the surface, the influence of patronage politics remained a significant force in personnel management. Jiang Zemin, who emerged as a surprising leader following the post-Tiananmen student movement, faced the crucial task of consolidating this leadership in the midst of various political competitors (Fewsmith 2021). As part of his strategy to secure his position, a substantial number of his personal secretaries, deputies, and close associates from Shanghai were elevated to top positions in the national hierarchy. This influential group included figures such as Zeng Qinghong, Wu Bangguo, Huang Ju, Chen Zhili, Wang Huning, Han Zheng, and Meng Jianzhu. Many of these individuals continued to wield significant influence long after Jiang formally stepped down from his leadership role. When Hu Jintao took the reins of power as planned in 2002, the Political Bureau was still dominated by Jiang's clients. However, Hu adopted a systematic approach to subvert this dominance. He mobilized his base within the CCYL and strategically placed many members in leading positions of local governments, such as provincial party secretaries and governors (Kou 2007). Notably, Li Keqiang, who would later become Hu's chosen successor, was one of these CCYL members. Hu's meticulous planning and execution proved effective, and by the time he passed the leadership baton to Xi Jinping, about a third of the Political Bureau had network ties to the CCYL and Hu (Fewsmith 2021). Moreover, there was a growing pipeline of CCYL associates who were being groomed for leadership positions. Many of these individuals were appointed as provincial party secretaries and governors. Li Keqiang also brough many of his former CCYL colleagues into the new State Council and appointed them as ministers and department chiefs.

It was generally expected that Xi Jinping would follow the footsteps of his predecessors and continue the established power arrangements while gradually asserting his dominance. To the surprise of many, Xi wasted no time in taking swift and decisive actions to eliminate the influence of his predecessors and establish his personal authority as the paramount figure within the Party as soon as he assumed office in 2012. In addition to implementing nationalist and populist policies, such as eradicating poverty, Xi targeted top state officials, criticizing many cadres for engaging in nepotism and pervasive corruption. During the fourth plenary meeting of the 18th Party Congress, Xi delivered his well-known remarks about seven "some people" within the Party, sending a stern warning that marked a significant shift in the Party's trajectory.

> Some individuals, ignoring the political discipline and rules of the party, do so for their own so-called career advancement and influence. Among them, there are those who practice favoritism, exclude dissenting voices, form cliques, and engage in factionalism. Some resort to anonymous accusations and the spread of rumors, while others manipulate public opinion and sway votes. Some make empty promises for personal gain, and some act against the party's principles while pretending otherwise. There are also those who boast about their own opinions while openly or secretly contradicting the party's central decisions (Xi 2014).

This characterization of the Party's cadre system is remarkably similar to the one issued by the Central Committee in 1986, as quoted earlier. Xi believed that this status quo was not acceptable. This diagnosis justified Xi's arrest of the new "Gang of Four" – Zhou Yongkang, Bo Xilai, Ling Jihua, and Xu Caihou. Many of their former personal secretaries, political allies, and family members were arrested and sentenced to lengthy prison terms. This political purge did not end with these high-profile cases. He wanted to purify the Party from inside out. Under the instruction of Xi, the Central Department of Organization carried out a large national survey and concluded that many local leaders "have knitted tight circles and built turfs (讲圈子、搞山头) in official appointments and some leaders promoted secretaries and close associates to leave backdoors open (留后路) after their retirement" (Central Department of Organization Party Building Institute 2014). Xi ordered the revision of *Regulations on the Selection and Appointment of Party and Government Leading Cadres* (Central Committee of the CCP 2002) and inserted a new principle of "appointing those who are virtuous and capable and from all corners of the world (五湖四海, 任人唯贤)," in addition to principles like the Party leading all cadre appointments.

Publicly denouncing factional politics and its adverse impact does not imply that Xi aimed to eradicate this practice and establish a merit-based cadre system. It primarily served as a pretext for eliminating rival political forces that could potentially challenge his effort to centralize power. Not unlike his predecessors, Xi showed a strong preference for appointing individuals closely aligned with him to fill all party and government positions. During the 19th Party Congress, only a handful of Jiang's loyalists and officials associated with the CCYL managed to retain their positions within the Political Bureau, even though they had diminished influence in the system and had little prospect for future career advancement. By the time the 20th Party Congress convened in 2022, they were all replaced, leaving Xi's former colleagues and allies in positions of significant influence at the highest echelons of central power. Instead of officials being selected from "all corners of the world," as promised in Xi's newly revised party regulations, the members of the new Politburo were remarkably similar in their backgrounds, including Xi's long-standing secretaries and subordinates from Zhejiang and Fujian provinces, as well as individuals connected through their shared professional backgrounds and familial bonds. In contrast to the factional mazework in previous Politburos, it is a sweeping victory for Xi's faction.

While the previous anecdotes may provoke interest and fascination, skeptics have valid concerns regarding the reliability of patronage affiliations, often based on subjective and arbitrary judgments made by some China observers or individuals claiming sources within the CCP. This research area has been shrouded in suspicion for decades. However, in recent years, there has been an increase in the availability of information about Chinese officials, making it feasible to systematically examine the patronage viewpoint.

One of the early studies that took a step in this direction was conducted by Shih, Adolph, and Liu (2012). They compiled a comprehensive biographic database of Central Committee officials from the 12th to the 16th Party Congress (1982–2007). To gauge these officials' relative standing in the bureaucratic hierarchy, they employed the latent rank ordering of these officials within the Central Committee. Theoretically, their relative standing is determined by the number of votes these members receive in elections, with higher vote-getters entering the more prestigious Central Committee positions and lower vote-getters serving as alternate members. In practice, this order is largely influenced by the top leaders, typically the General Party Secretary and other members of the PSC, who can utilize the Party's organizational infrastructure and disciplinary mechanisms to ensure that the final votes align with their preferences.

If the patronage argument holds true, officials with stronger patronage ties should be ranked higher within the Central Committee. For the 16th Party Congress, Shih, Adolph, and Liu (2012) found that officials with birthplace, college, and workplace ties to Deng Xiaoping continued to enjoy certain privileges, with an average rank 14 percentile points higher than the average member, even though Deng had passed away five years prior. Hu Jintao had just assumed the role of General Party Secretary, but his CCYL faction already had a 7-percentile rank advantage over the average member, indicating Hu Jintao's involvement in personnel arrangements before formally taking office. Surprisingly, Central Committee members with ties to the departing General Party Secretary, Jiang Zemin, did not exhibit any noticeable advantage. According to the authors, this was a consequence of Jiang Zemin's tendency to overpromote his household staff, who were often far less qualified for high positions compared to the average Central Committee members. When examining other time periods, the study found that Hu Yaobang similarly promoted his faction members vigorously, whereas Zhao Ziyang was less inclined to elevate his affiliates to higher positions in the Central Committee. Some results (Deng's oversized influence and Zhao's minimal impact) align with anecdotes and case studies in previous literature, while others (Jiang's ambiguous influence) seem to contradict conventional views. Despite some uncertainty in these results, they offer the first systematic evidence that largely supports the patronage hypothesis.

The Central Committee is often considered the apex of the ruling circle, where political dynamics are distinct and significant emphasis is placed on political loyalty with the top elite. In contrast, regional politics tends to prioritize economic and social developments, requiring promotions based on tangible achievements rather than wasteful nepotism. To test whether patronage politics is less prevalent in the regional dimension, Opper, Nee, and Brehm (2015) take the patronage hypothesis directly to the promotion of provincial leaders. Despite attempting to differentiate their homophilic connection concept from patronage and political factions, their empirical measures align with those in Shih, Adolph, and Liu (2012). Officials with homophily ties are identified based on birthplace, college, and workplace overlaps with members of the PSC. Their promotion criteria, however, deviate from the common practice in the literature and exclude advancements to some deputy national leadership positions, including the State Councilors, members of the CCP's Secretariat, the Chief Justice of the Supreme Court, and so on. Despite this rather unconventional choice, their study, analyzing 353 provincial leaders from 1979 to 2011, reveals statistically significant effects on promotion when politically connected to higher-ups. This conclusion is robust to adding year and region fixed effects in the regression models, and other individual-level covariates. Their study lends more credibility to the claim that patronage is a pervasive phenomenon throughout the Chinese state, not limited to the Central Committee.

Numerous scholars have expanded on these promising works and reported additional supportive evidence for factionalism within different segments of the Chinese party-state across different time periods. However, two recent papers have arrived at starkly opposing conclusions. At first glance, the papers by

Francois, Trebbi, and Xiao (2023) and Fisman et al. (2020) seem quite similar, both seeking to test the patronage and factionalism argument and focusing on the Central Committee of the CCP. Yet their findings diverge significantly. On the one hand, Francois, Trebbi, and Xiao (2023) affirm the powerful impact of factions in official promotions, aligning with prior literature. According to their estimates, having patronage ties can increase an official's promotion chances by 10 percent. They further quantify that among all Politburo leaders, the Standing Committee members command 75 percent of total influence, leaving the remainder for regular members. In contrast, Fisman et al. (2020) report a "connection penalty." According to their findings, having ties with Politburo members actually diminishes a Central Committee member's likelihood of being promoted to the Politburo, reducing it by 5 to 9 percentage points.

A closer examination of their methodologies reveals subtle yet crucial differences between these two studies. Firstly, their datasets cover different time periods. Francois, Trebbi, and Xiao (2023) include the 11th to the 18th Central Committees, while Fisman et al. (2020) expand the coverage from the 8th to the 19th Central Committees. Given Mao's unusual emphasis on combating factionalism, the negative finding in Fisman et al. (2020) likely reflects their inclusion of Mao's Central Committees. Secondly, their measurements of factionalism and patronage differ significantly. While Fisman et al. (2020) follow the conventional approach of identifying personal ties between a Politburo member and a Central Committee member based on personal linkages through birthplace, college, and work experience, Francois, Trebbi, and Xiao (2023) code factional ties as 1 if a Central Committee member has worked in the CCYL offices, in Shanghai, in the military, or is a descendent of senior party leaders. These are distinct approaches. The first captures direct, dyadic, and personal connections between patrons (usually members in the Politburo or in senior positions in the bureaucratic hierarchy) and clients (usually members in the Central Committee or in junior positions in the bureaucratic hierarchy). The second is an indication of belonging to certain organizational or social circles, without direct reference to a patron–client relationship. Finally, in their regression models, Francois, Trebbi, and Xiao (2023) control only individual attributes, bureaucratic rank fixed effects, and year fixed effects. Fisman et al. (2020) assert that this approach, shared by other previous works, has made a mistake in not controlling for group (birthplace and college) fixed effects. They argue that these studies incorrectly attribute the effect of qualities associated with these entities, such as high competence of Tsinghua University graduates, to personal ties. After adding these fixed effects to their regressions, Fisman et al. (2020) found that factional tie variables turned negative.

To what extent do these differences in data range, measurements, and modeling choices explain their opposing findings? More empirical research in the future should add more light to this important debate. But there is an important message for all researchers in this field: these methodological issues must be taken seriously to make real progress, a point we will discuss in great detail in the critical evaluation section of this Element (Section 3).

2.2 Formal Rules and Performance-Based Meritocracy

Setting aside internal struggles among elite factions, power holders in autocracies must also address the threat of uprisings from the general population. This necessitates the presence of capable officials who can improve the regime's governance and gain popular approval, as suggested by Boix and Svolik (2013). According to proponents of this opposing camp, during the era of Mao's loyalists, the national economy was in such dire straits that Deng openly acknowledged that the CCP would cease to exist unless people's living standards improved. He set in motion a transformation from a revolutionary regime to a modernizing state and reoriented elite recruitment from loyalty to competence (Lee 1991). Young officials, being energetic and more open-minded toward new ideas, were given priorities in promotion. Additionally, mandatory retirement ages were also introduced to make room for fresh blood at all levels of the state apparatus. Rather than prioritizing impeccable class backgrounds and political loyalty, individuals with advanced degrees in fields such as science, technology, economics, and management found themselves on a fast track to higher positions. Beyond age and education requirements, the post-Mao leadership further emphasized that officials must ascend the bureaucratic ladder in a step-by-step fashion, gaining essential administrative experience and building governing credentials starting from grassroots levels (Central Committee of the CCP 1986).

These standards and requirements have undoubtedly bolstered the level of institutionalization in cadre management and improved the overall quality of the officials within the Chinese state. However, proponents of the meritocratic view take it a step further and contend that the specific approach to the Party's management of cadre promotions has ushered in a truly meritocratic regime. According to these analysts, in the post-Mao era, the central leadership has thrust all local officials into fierce competitions with their peers and selected the top performers for promotion (Blanchard and Shleifer 2001). Performance is measured by various quantifiable targets, but it all boils down to economic growth rates in their jurisdictions because most social and economic indicators are highly dependent on regional economic development levels (Oi 1999;

Whiting 2006). Unlike the traditional U-form organizational structure in the Soviet Union, economic reforms and fiscal decentralization since the 1980s have granted local officials significant control over resource allocation and the authority to formulate policies for regional economic development. According to Qian and Xu (1993), this M-form organizational structure is ideal to enable the central government to conduct yardstick competition. Because these jurisdictions are roughly comparable (either across geographic regions or across time periods for one region), high growth can be considered a reliable indicator of the competence of their respective leaders. In other words, when regions experience high growth, it can be inferred that the leading officials in charge must have adopted effective policies and pursued growth-fostering strategies. In theory, these top-down and systematic cadre evaluations can serve a role analogous to competitive elections in a democratic system. One could even argue that these performance reviews are potentially more scientific and objective than the subjective judgments of voters, offering a more reliable basis for meritocracy compared to often unpredictable elections (Bell 2016).

The evidence for such a meritocratic system seems to be quite strong. Over the course of several decades, the CCP has engaged in extensive experimentation and rule-making, resulting in the creation of an increasingly sophisticated cadre management system. Table 1 compiles key central documents in this regard. Documents on the left were sanctioned and promulgated by the Central Committee of the CCP, the highest governing body of the Party. In terms of regulating leading officials' selection and appointment, one significant development was the 1986 notice to the country, which marked a turning point in the Party's approach to cadre selection. It formally acknowledged the need to depart from the traditional Maoist cadre system, which was often characterized by loyalty and revolutionary zeal. Instead, the notice introduced a set of general principles for official appointments, including personal qualifications such as age, education, and work experience. These criteria were intended to identify individuals with the skills and knowledge necessary to navigate the challenges of a rapidly modernizing China. The transition from general principles to actionable procedures and rules was marked by the 1995 interim provision, which laid down the practical steps for vetting candidates and deciding cadre choices. The 2002 party regulation solidified these criteria, becoming the cornerstone of cadre appointment at both central and local government levels. The importance of this regulation is underscored by the fact that Xi Jinping, in his endeavors to tighten control over personnel decisions in the Party, directed two revisions to the regulation in 2014 and 2019.

In order to base personnel decisions on a more scientific foundation, the Central Department of Organization was tasked with developing and implementing a cadre

Table 1 Central party documents regulating leadership selection, appointment and assessment

Selection and appointment	Year	Assessment
	1979	*Opinions on Implementing a Cadre Assessment System* Central Department of Organization 1979
Notice from the Central Committee of the Communist Party of China on Strictly Selecting and Appointing Cadres in Accordance with Party Principles Central Committee of the CCP 1986	1986	
	1988	*Annual Work Assessment Scheme (Trial) for County (City, District) Party and Government Leading Cadres* Central Department of Organization 1988
Interim Provisions on the Selection and Appointment of Party and Government Leading Cadres Central Committee of the CCP 1995	1995	
	1998	*Interim Provisions on the Assessment of Party and Government Leading Cadres* Central Department of Organization 1998
Regulations on the Selection and Appointment of Party and Government Leading Cadres Central Committee of the CCP 2002	2002	
	2006	*Comprehensive Assessment and Evaluation Measures for Local Party and Government Leadership Teams and Cadres in Accordance with the Requirements of the Scientific Development Concept* Central Department of Organization 2006
	2009	*Local Party and Government Leadership Team and Cadre Comprehensive Assessment and Evaluation Method (Trial)* Central Department of Organization 2009b

Table 1 (cont.)

Selection and appointment	Year	Assessment
	2009	*Annual Assessment Method for Party and Government Leadership Teams and Cadres (Trial)* Central Department of Organization 2009a
Regulations on the Selection and Appointment of Party and Government Leading Cadres Central Committee of the CCP 2014	2014	
Regulations on the Selection and Appointment of Party and Government Leading Cadres Central Committee of the CCP 2019	2019	*Regulations on the Assessment of Party and Government Leading Cadres* General Office of the Central Committee of the CCP 2019

Sources: Authors' collection from various party and government websites, including www.cpcnews.cn, www.gov.cn, www.gongwei.org.cn, and www.12371.cn.

evaluation system that relies on quantitative measures. The essential regulations and documents related to this initiative are summarized on the right side of Table 1. In 1979, during a National Party Organizational Department Conference, the matter of cadre assessment was officially introduced as a significant responsibility for all the Departments of Organization across the country. However, it was not until 1988 that the Central Department of Organization rolled out its pilot policy, with a primary focus on county-level leading officials, which included party secretaries, magistrates, and standing committee members of county party committees. The introductory statement of this policy was explicit in its aim to motivate officials to compete based on real work achievements, or "实绩." To standardize the assessment process, the Central Department of Organization even provided some predefined forms for use. Following feedback from these trials, a provisional regulation was established in 1998 and applied to all leading members of the Party and the state. This regulation reinforced the importance of real work achievements and outlined various quantitative criteria that should be considered in these assessments, with economic growth rate and fiscal revenue growth topping the list. While Hu Jintao sought to promote a scientific development concept that prioritized people's well-being within the party, the regulations issued during his tenure in 2006 and 2009 incorporated economic development metrics on a per capita basis, in addition to aggregate figures. Nevertheless, the emphasis on economic and fiscal revenue growth remained prominent in these documents. Furthermore, the directives instructed evaluators to judge regional leaders in comparison to their counterparts in other jurisdictions and their own past performance during a single term. The 2009 annual evaluation method went a step further, mandating that a minimum of two candidates be considered for each promotion position, intensifying the competitive pressure on local cadres.

In accordance with these existing rules, the cadre evaluation system comprises four distinct types of assessment.[1] Regular assessments (平时考核) serve to monitor the day-to-day activities of leading officials, while specialized assessments (专项考核) evaluate their performance in specific tasks and their handling of critical emergencies. The results of these assessments are often included in the personal records of these leaders and contribute to their overall performance evaluations. Term assessments (任期考核) provide a comprehensive evaluation of cadres' performance during their tenure in office. Given that many leaders leave their positions before their terms expire, term assessments are typically integrated into their annual assessments (年度考核). As a result, proponents of the meritocratic perspective tend to place greater emphasis on annual assessments. The Central Department of Organization has established detailed procedures for these annual assessments in its various regulations. Individual leaders are rated as "excellent," "competent," "basically competent," or "incompetent" based on their annual performance. Promotion to higher offices is primarily granted to those who achieve an "excellent" rating. Individuals rated as "basically competent" may be required to engage in admonition review sessions with their superiors, while those deemed "incompetent" often face demotion or removal from their current positions.

The Departments of Organization at various levels have translated these central directives to implementable policies in their respective jurisdictions. As an illustration, in 2021 the Gansu Provincial Party Committee conducted annual assessments of cadres under its purview, including 305 leadership groups and 2,038 leading officials. The result revealed that 98.36 percent of leadership groups and 98.92 percent of leading officials were rated as "excellent" or "competent." Leaders in the "excellent" category were primarily selected from cities and counties with "advanced" or "strong" economies (Gansu Provincial Department of Organization 2023). As a reward for their outstanding performance, the Department of Organization officials pledged financial rewards and increased prospects of promotion for those consistently rated as "excellent" for three consecutive years. Looking ahead, the Party Committee planned to

---

[1] Diverse assessments are administered by a range of central ministries and departments, with the core objective of pressing local government and party agencies at every tier to fulfill their mandated duties from the central government. Our primary focus here pertains exclusively to assessments carried out by the Departments of Organization, specifically targeting leading officials across various administrative levels.

introduce specialized assessments for leading cadres in fourteen cities, with a focus on their ability to attract investment to their regions, thereby emphasizing the importance of "investment attraction and business development" as a heroic endeavor (Gansu Provincial Department of Organization 2023).

Quantitative measures are more widely used at the lower levels of the state hierarchy. In 2006, the Wenzhou Municipal Party Committee in Zhejiang Province, for example, categorized the real work achievements of county-level cadres into two main groups: economic targets and political and social targets. They assigned specific numerical values to each task to evaluate the performance of these cadres. For instance, economic targets included measures like GDP and its growth rate (nine points), fiscal revenue and its growth rate (nine points), fixed investment and its growth rate (six points), among eighteen economic subcategories. These economic targets collectively held a total weight of fifty-two points. On the other hand, political and social targets encompassed fourteen categories, such as social stability (seven points), public health (five points), and birth control (five points), totaling forty-eight points (Tao, Liu, and Hou 2020).

In the same year, the Cangzhou Municipal Party Committee in Hebei Province applied a similar formula to assess the real work achievements of its county-level cadres. Instead of assigning different values to each subcategory, it allocated 8.3 points to six key economic targets – GDP per capita and its growth rate, fiscal revenue per capita and its growth rate, fixed investment, investment from other regions, international exports, and net income of urban and rural residents – and their respective growth rates. Additionally, it assigned 2.7 points to each of the eighteen categories within political and social targets, covering areas like local party development, grassroots democracy, religion and minority affairs, public security, social stability, environmental protection, and birth control, among others. Mengcun County within Cangzhou Municipality followed a similar framework but made slight adjustments by eliminating irrelevant categories and increasing the weight of fiscal revenue to twelve points, along with setting fixed investment and outside investment to ten points (Tao, Liu, and Hou 2020). It is important to note that each regional party committee might tailor the specific targets and their relative weights to suit their local needs. Nevertheless, all leading cadres in these areas were evaluated based on measurable objectives and received merit ratings for their real work accomplishments.

Apart from utilizing documentary evidence and case studies, scholars have also dedicated substantial efforts to empirically test the meritocratic argument using systematic data. This endeavor has been made feasible due to the increasing availability of biographical information concerning Chinese officials.

Various research institutions have been amassing such data for decades, and recent transparency initiatives by the CCP have further facilitated this trend. The first published work in this regard is Bo's 1996 study on the mobility of provincial leaders. He compiled information on all provincial party secretaries and governors from 1949 to 1994. To gauge officials' individual abilities, he employed two economic performance indicators: the average economic growth rate and the average fiscal revenue contributions to the central government during the officials' tenure. His findings indicated that strong economic performance reduced the risk of officials being demoted, which supports the meritocratic perspective. However, he also observed that superior economic performance among these provincial leaders actually decreased their chances of promotion to higher positions. Clearly, the Party did not appear to reward provincial officials whose performance indicated higher competence. The official endorsement of meritocracy in the CCP's cadre policy did not occur until Deng's rise to power. In fact, Mao actively discouraged officials who prioritized expertise and economic achievements over their commitment to communist ideology and personal loyalty to him. Therefore, this empirical test does not do justice to the meritocracy thesis if data from 1949 onward are pooled together.

Maskin, Qian, and Xu (2000) developed the meritocratic thesis formally in a model and argued that Chinese central leaders utilized yardstick competition as a means to promote regional leaders. To substantiate their thesis, they employed a province's per capita count of Central Committee members within the highest governing body of the CCP as a proxy for promotion. An increase in a province's relative rank was viewed as a form of promotion for that province. They measured performance by comparing the relative rank of provincial GDP growth rates across the country for two time periods: the 11th Party Congress in 1977 and the 13th Party Congress in 1987. This design allowed them to assess the direct impact of changing cadre selection criteria, something not possible in Bo (1996). Their findings indicated that as a province's relative rank in economic growth improved from 1977 to 1987, its relative rank in the Central Committee also saw positive changes. However, the study has a significant limitation in that it chooses provinces as the basic unit of analysis, whereas central documents clearly emphasize rewarding individual leaders' performance rather than administrative units. Additionally, their regression analysis shows only the correlation between these two variables and lacks effective controls for other provincial-level factors that influence Central Committee representations, such as economic development, ethnic minority status, and administrative ranks. The normalization of the number of Central Committee members by population size also raises questions, as these positions are typically allocated relatively equitably to all provincial units, more akin to the US Senate rather than the House of Representatives.

Li and Zhou (2005) expanded upon the preliminary findings of Maskin, Qian, and Xu (2000) by subjecting the meritocratic perspective to a more rigorous examination. Instead of using provincial ranking in the Central Committee as a proxy for promotion, they directly analyzed career changes of provincial leaders and their association with economic performance. Unlike Bo (1996), they narrowed their data range to the years between 1979 and 1995. For provincial leaders, ascending to a new position within the national elite (such as the Party's Political Bureau, the State Council, etc.) was considered a promotion. Economic performance was gauged by the province's annual growth rate and the average GDP growth during the leader's tenure. This empirical approach allowed for the inclusion of control variables at the individual level, such as age, education, tenure, and central government experience. Ordered probit regressions revealed that the economic performance of leaders, in terms of both annual and moving GDP growth rates, exerted significant and substantial impacts on their likelihood of advancing to the highest echelons. This suggests that post-Mao leadership very likely prioritized individual merit in its personnel management system.

In a related study, Chen, Li, and Zhou (2005) updated the data to the year 2002. Furthermore, they adjusted the performance metrics, enabling superiors to explicitly compare leaders with their peers in neighboring provinces and their immediate predecessors in the same region. This design closely aligned with the yardstick competition assumption. Once again, their results demonstrated robust and statistically significant effects of economic performance. This affirmed the additional requirement of comparing actual achievements across different regions and within the same term, as mandated by the Central Department of Organization in its 2006 assessment document. While these findings were subsequently challenged in Tao et al. (2010), their results sparked significant interest, especially among economists, in further exploring this research avenue. If the Chinese state has rewarded its political leaders with higher competence through more prestigious positions, as these scholars argue, it makes sense that local governments are the "helping hands" behind China's rapid economic growth.

2.3 Summary

This section shows that there exists a substantial body of theoretical, anecdotal, and statistical research supporting both sides of the debate. Recognizing the inherent trade-offs between competence and loyalty, certain scholars argue that different segments within the state hierarchy may adopt varying cadre selection rules. These dynamics can also shift depending on specific leaders at the helm and varying time periods. We will revisit these claims about heterogeneous promotion rules in the empirical section. However, it is pertinent to mention a lesser-discussed perspective within the literature. Jia, Kudamatsu, and Seim (2015) challenge the prevailing views and contend that these two principles are not necessarily mutually exclusive. They propose that, for a country as expansive as China, the top leader possesses a unique advantage in reconciling competence and loyalty by fostering tournament-style competition among loyal adherents. This approach addresses the ruler's political survival concerns and facilitates the appointment of capable leaders to pivotal positions, thereby promoting accelerated economic growth. While this viewpoint presents an intriguing alternative, it requires further theoretical elaboration, especially in light of the loyalty–competence trade-off. From an empirical standpoint, aside from the aforementioned scholars, other studies have not successfully replicated statistically significant effects related to the interaction between patronage and performance. Consequently, we do not exclusively highlight this minority perspective but instead concentrate on the two predominant viewpoints in this literature review.

3 Meritocracy in One-Party China? A Critical Evaluation

The theoretical framework of patronage and factionalism has long been a cornerstone in the analysis of CCP politics. While recent systematic and quantitative studies have bolstered the credibility of this viewpoint, it remains subject to robust challenges, mostly concerning its empirical methods. Consequently, its impact on political economists has been somewhat subdued. Conversely, the meritocratic view has rapidly gained favor, particularly among quantitatively oriented political economists. The notion of officials seeking promotion under meritocratic rules has become a standard modeling assumption, influencing a myriad theoretical and empirical works examining diverse aspects of the Chinese political economy. These include studies on official mobilities and their impacts on firms' investment behavior (An et al. 2016; Xu, Qian, and Li 2013), urban spatial planning and land finance (Wang, Zhang, and Zhou 2020), housing price fluctuations (Liu, Huang, and Wang 2018; Zhu and Xu 2013), as well as the phenomenon of political business and fiscal cycles (Gong, Xiao, and Zhang 2017; Mei, Wang, and Lei 2014; Tsai 2016).

This section critically assesses the meritocratic perspective, offering a series of critiques and elucidating why it may not be the most apt model for understanding Chinese political economy in the post-Mao era. A primary theoretical challenge surfaces, as proponents of the meritocratic approach struggle to provide a cogent explanation for the compatibility of a meritocratic system within the confines of a one-party political framework. By placing power at the forefront of its model, the patronage argument captures the fundamental intricacies of Chinese elite politics and shows more potential as a fitting lens for analyzing China's political economy. Moreover, advocates of the meritocratic viewpoint have misrepresented China's cadre management system, thereby weakening the factual foundation of the meritocratic view. Lastly, we delve into a methodological challenge that confronts all quantitative studies on elite mobility, underscoring the complexities inherent in this analytical approach.

3.1 Theoretical Inadequacy

The meritocratic view presents a refreshing perspective in the realm of autocratic politics. Over the decades, researchers examining autocratic political systems have grappled with the complexity and ambiguity inherent in such political landscapes. Unlike scholars studying democratic politics who can utilize elections to simplify their modeling of politicians and deduce policy and economic consequences, those exploring autocratic political economy face the challenges of informal dynamics and a lack of clear and transparent rules. From this standpoint, the meritocratic argument introduces a streamlined mechanism akin to elections in the study of democratic political economy, offering a welcome departure from the inherent messiness of autocratic politics. This focus on official incentives proves particularly desirable for the advancement of the discipline, as evidenced by the surge in political-economic research cited already. However, it is crucial to note a theoretical risk associated with this approach, namely, the potential for conflating politicians with bureaucrats – a peril cautioned against by some noted scholars in the study of the political economy of the state: "In much of the political economy literature, the two are bundled together as 'government', but they often perform different roles and are subject to different accountability mechanisms. Better understanding of these roles, both theoretically and empirically, is an important area for future research in developing countries" (Besley et al. 2021: 30). This cautionary note is applicable to the wider field of political economy but holds particular relevance for students studying Chinese political economy. Under China's one-party rule, the boundary between the state and the Party becomes considerably blurred. Most high-ranking cadres begin their careers as office clerks within government or party organizations. They subsequently transition across party and state entities throughout their professional trajectories, eventually ascending to leading official positions of the Party or the state at different levels. It might be reasonable to consider non-leadership cadres as bureaucrats whose career advancement depends on their abilities to fulfill tasks as determined by their superiors. However, the meritocracy model extends this conceptualization to all leading cadres, particularly those governing regional entities. While there are certainly overlaps between politicians and bureaucrats in the real world, there are also clear conceptual differences. Unlike bureaucrats, politicians must define policy objectives and are consequently held accountable for the outcomes, facing rewards or punishments based on their choices. On the other hand, bureaucrats lack the discretion to formulate policies; their role is confined to implementing them. Consequently, they cannot claim credit for policies or be penalized for them.

Recognizing the difference between politicians and bureaucrats, the decision to extend the bureaucratic analogy to leading local officials raises questions. The meritocracy model operates on the assumption that local officials wield significant power due to decentralization in the reform era. This assumption suggests that these officials possess the autonomy to shape policies and influence economic and social outcomes in their respective domains, seemingly contradicting the bureaucratic model. However, the proponents could argue that while local governments have gained more authority in economic matters, the center has recentralized the personnel system. Consequently, all leading officials must look upward for career advancement, resembling the hierarchy within a bureaucratic organization (Blanchard and Shleifer 2001; Xu 2011). This portrayal is somewhat misleading because, in reality, the Chinese cadre system has undergone decentralization in the post-Mao era. In 1984, the Party shifted cadre management from a two-level-down approach to a one-level-down approach, granting officials more authority over personnel decisions about subordinates directly below them, a power previously controlled from two levels up. Additionally, as part of the efforts to regularize Chinese politics, leading government and party officials are required to secure enough votes in elections within their respective Party Congresses and People's Congresses. Despite considerable party controls from above, some cadres have indeed lost these elections. In order to avoid failure and shame in a public fashion, these leading cadres must look downwards to seek support from local representatives, typically rank-and-file members in their regional establishments. Moreover, the proponents of meritocracy tend to downplay a crucial aspect, whether intentionally or inadvertently: one original goal of introducing cadre assessments was to institutionalize peer reviews of leading cadres. This new system gives peers occupying similar hierarchical levels and their immediate subordinates a formal role in key personnel decisions. While this will be elaborated further in a section about cadre assessment, it suffices here to highlight that the notion that China adopted a highly centralized cadre management system, thereby justifying the treatment of all leading officials as centrally controlled bureaucrats, lacks conceptual justification.

This conceptual issue holds significant implications for the analysis of power. When viewed through a bureaucratic lens, governance appears reduced to a mere exercise in scientific management, mechanistic and procedural. While administrative efficiency and rational decision-making might indeed bolster the regime's overall productivity, this perspective fails to address a more fundamental question: Why would an autocrat aim to establish and maintain a Weberian state? A Weberian state, characterized by its rational-legal authority and adherence to formal rules and procedures, might seem beneficial for administrative efficiency. However, an autocrat's primary concern is not merely streamlined governance but the consolidation and perpetuation of their power. By adopting a merit-based rating system that objectively measures and discloses each leader's performance and merit, the autocrat effectively surrenders their discretion in personnel arrangements. However, the essence of autocratic power lies in the freedom from constraints, especially concerning official appointments. While autocracy may appear calm on the surface, power struggles persistently threaten the stability of the regime. Leaders at the top must consistently grapple with challenges from political rivals. To ensure their survival, they must retain the autonomy to appoint loyal supporters, irrespective of their merit ratings. This discretion is pivotal for their enduring hold on power.

It might be argued that the autocrat could use the merit rating as a partial input while reserving final say over personnel decisions. After all, why couldn't the autocrat select officials who rank highly in both merit and loyalty? Wouldn't that be ideal for the autocrat? However, such a system would cease to be truly meritocratic by definition. Moreover, this viewpoint overlooks the inherent contradiction between competence and loyalty. For some scholars, loyalty is an intrinsic trait, something like a person's innate ability to reason. These two attributes are orthogonal, meaning that an autocrat can pick competent followers for economic growth in normal circumstances and when political survival is endangered select both competent and loyal followers. This conceptualization oversimplifies matters. As Egorov and Sonin (2011) argue, there are no inherently loyal or disloyal individuals; loyalty is a choice made when individuals are presented with competing offers for their services. To make this issue more problematic in autocratic politics, if an autocrat appoints certain clients to higher positions, these individuals automatically possess more resources and privileges in their hands due to the unchecked power in autocratic states. This can lead to potentially undesirable consequences. Increased resources elevate these officials' power ambition and embolden them to eye for higher positions, including the autocrat's own power. Even if these individuals do not actively seek more power, their heightened status can be perceived as threatening by the autocrat. Mao's strained relationship with his handpicked successors is a notable example. On the flip side, political rivals may be enticed to offer better incentives to win over them and strengthen their hands in the political fight. The irony is that competent officials are more susceptible to the temptation of betrayal because of the higher values they can bring to the rivals as well as their ability to leverage status and resources more effectively. As a result, a power-conscious autocrat would naturally favor less-competent officials in return for greater loyalty.

Supporters of the meritocratic perspective might still argue that China's embrace of a meritocratic state was born out of a unique opportunity. Following Mao's death, the Chinese economy lay in ruins due to the ravages of Mao and his radical loyalists during the Cultural Revolution. This dire situation put the very survival of the CCP in question. Deng Xiaoping consistently emphasized this urgency to the Party leadership. In the preparatory meeting for the significant 3rd Plenary Session of the 11th Party Congress in December 1978, Deng sounded a stern warning: "a party, a country, or a nation that solely relies on ideological dogma from books [by Mao], adheres to rigid thoughts, and holds on to superstitions, cannot advance. Such rigidity halts progress and vitality, leading to the demise of both the party and the nation" (Deng 1978). He urged unity within the Party to embark on a new journey toward achieving the four modernizations and lifting China out of its backwardness. According to these advocates, even though the top elites were still keen on jostling for power, they must first embrace a merit-based system for their collective survival.

Upon closer examination, this line of reasoning does not hold up for two primary reasons. Firstly, while it is widely accepted that the Chinese economy was in a dire situation following Mao's death, there exists a possibility that this was no more than strategic political maneuvering, not a factual description of the reality. Eisenman (2018) meticulously investigated the productivity of communes across various regions in the 1970s and found no compelling evidence indicating an imminent economic crisis. On the contrary, agricultural productivity, life expectancy, and basic education in rural areas significantly improved under the commune system. This improvement was attributed to several factors, including investments in agricultural technology, economies of scale, and the diversification of the rural economy after China's normalization with the West in 1972 and the ensuing weakened military pressure. The commune system also facilitated China's adoption of the Green Revolution, allowing for the widespread introduction of hybrid seeds, fertilizers, mechanization, and irrigation. Another recent study on the productivity of the Household Responsibility System lends more credibility to this revisionist reading of China's reform history. Utilizing satellite imagery, Ferguson and Kim (2023) estimated agricultural productivity by analyzing light reflection from plants. This approach helped avoid potential manipulation in local government production statistics. Their results did not confirm the alleged beneficial impact of the Household Responsibility System on rural productivity either. However, political motives intervened. Deng Xiaoping and his supporters initiated an ideological debate framed as a discussion on the merit of productivity to undermine the legitimacy of Mao's successor and his commitment to this system. Their objective was to oust their political adversaries and consolidate their own political dominance. This strategy proved effective, as Hua Guofeng and his allies were swiftly marginalized following this maneuvering.

Secondly, this belief rests on a rather simplistic understanding of economic development. While it is true that economic reforms and development may elevate the aggregate level of wealth of a society, the distribution of newly created wealth is never politically impartial. Moore's (1993 [1966]) seminal study of modernization in Britain, France, and Germany illustrates how the emerging industrial class reaped the benefits of laissez-faire policies, marketization, and capitalism. Concurrently, traditional groups like landlords and nobles, deeply rooted in rural economies, saw a gradual erosion of their societal and political standing. These shifts led to the ascension of the bourgeoisie and the decline of nobility's influence in politics. A similar dynamic unfolded in late Qing court politics. Conservatives were held back by their adherence to cultural values and Confucian beliefs. However, it was evident that they were also wary of giving reformers the opportunity to engage in trade with foreign countries and establish domestic industries. They feared that this would bolster the resources of their political rivals and weaken their own influence within the court. Likewise, post-Mao reforms had distributional consequences for different elite camps at the top echelon. Intense debates in the 1980s and 1990s about socialism and the general direction of economic reforms were driven by concerns among figures like Chen Yun and Li Peng, fearing implications for their power bases in the state planning apparatus and the state-owned sector. Jiang Zemin's extensive patronage networks in banking, financial services, real estate, high-tech, and security apparatus drew envy and suspicion from Xi Jinping, prompting him to target and restrict the growth of these sectors (Fewsmith 2021). Overall economic growth hardly served as a unifying force among power-driven elites during the reform era. In reality, economic reform policies became battlegrounds deeply entangled in power struggles among the top leadership.

3.2 Factual Misrepresentation

Table 1 showcases a series of resolutions and regulations from the Central Committee and the Central Department of Organization, indicating the CCP's dedication to reforming its cadre management system. These efforts aim to institutionalize and enhance the system's scientific basis. We do not question the existence of such a system or deny that real work achievements are being used in this system. However, it is crucial to address misconceptions propagated by proponents of the meritocratic view regarding China's evolving cadre assessment system. We raise three basic factual questions here: What specific aspects of cadres' performance are being assessed and quantified? Is there a formal link between assessment results and subsequent promotions? Is there a nationally uniform cadre assessment system?

3.2.1 What Is Assessed?

Readers of the meritocracy literature often get the impression that economic outcomes, particularly GDP growth rate, predominantly dictate cadre performance reviews. Some researchers may include fiscal revenue growth rates and total regional investments in the list. These are highly correlated with the overall economic growth. Many advocates of this viewpoint also like to quote a warning from the Central Committee of the CCP against assessing cadres' performance "based solely on regional GDP and growth rankings" and use it to support the claim that "GDP worship" is a pervasive practice in cadre assessment (General Office of the Central Committee of the CCP 2019). What is conveniently omitted from the well-known quote is the rest of the statement. Article 29, where the quote originates, actually reads as follows:

> The determination of assessment results should emphasize strengthened comprehensive analysis and judgment, adhering to a combination of qualitative and quantitative approaches. It should involve a comprehensive, historical, and dialectical analysis of individual contributions and collective actions, subjective

efforts, and objective conditions, growth rates versus quality benefits, visible achievements and potential achievements, as well as the outcomes of development versus incurred costs. It's important to focus on understanding the genuine sentiments and evaluations of the people towards economic and social development, preventing the simplistic determination of assessment results based solely on regional GDP rankings, growth rates, democratic evaluations, or opinion poll scores. (General Office of the Central Committee of the CCP 2019)

This quote highlights that, in many regions, cadre performance evaluations also rely exclusively on "democratic evaluations or opinion poll scores." To fully comprehend this statement, it is crucial to understand the actual process of cadre assessment. In 2009, to establish a scientific framework for cadre assessment, the Central Department of Organization issued specific guidelines on evaluating cadres.

Table 2, a form taken from the *Annual Assessment Method for Party and Government Leadership Teams and Cadres (Trial)* (Central Department of Organization 2009a), reveals that the performance of senior officials is assessed across five primary categories: virtue, ability, diligence, achievement, and integrity. Contrary to the emphasis placed solely on real work achievement by the meritocratic perspective, the achievement is just one component among these five.

More significantly, the evaluation of their performance doesn't rely on objective and scientific benchmarks but rather on subjective rankings. As per the cadre assessment regulation, the pertinent Department of Organization responsible for the assessment must gather all peers at the equivalent administrative level as the officials under review, along with their immediate subordinates. These individuals then assess the leaders' performance using a grading system: excellent (A), competent (B), basically competent (C), and incompetent (D) on the assessment form. For instance, Yueyang City in Hunan Province is on schedule to conduct its annual assessment of county-level leaders, like party secretaries. The ultimate assessors would be the party secretary and other members of the Yueyang Municipal Party Standing Committee. They would direct the municipal Department of Organization to conduct "democratic evaluations sessions" in all counties. Notably, leading members of the county party committees, governments, People's Congresses (PCs), and People's Political Consultative Conferences (PPCCs) such as deputy party secretaries, county party standing committee members, county magistrates, deputy magistrates, chairmen, and vice chairmen of the PCs and PPCCs, are convened in each county for a session on democratic evaluation. Additionally invited to participate are leading cadres in county party and government departments, like the Department of Propaganda

Table 2 An evaluation form of leading cadres in democratic assessment sessions

Name	Overall	Virtue 德	Ability 能	Diligence 勤	Achievement 绩	Integrity 廉
		Political steadfastness	Work strategy	Spiritual condition and dedication to work	Completing annual tasks	Integrity and self-discipline
		Implementing democratic centralism	Managing the team and leading the personnel		Solving major issues	Fulfilling anti-corruption responsibilities
		Adherence to principles	Maintaining stability		Emphasizing long-term development	
		Moral qualities				
xxx	A	A	A	A	A	A
	B	B	B	B	B	B
	C	C	C	C	C	C
	D	D	D	D	D	D

Source: Central Department of Organization 2009a.

and the Bureau of Finance, among others, along with leading cadres in township positions. These people fill in an assessment form akin to Table 3. Similar to the Central Department of Organization form, the county party secretaries are graded by virtue, ability, diligence, achievement, and integrity. An aggregate category summarizes their overall performance as evaluated by the participants. This final grade, presented as percentages of votes in each category, becomes a crucial part of the cadre's annual assessment report (Table 4).

It is important to note that, while evaluations of this nature are inherently subjective, the achievement category holds a more objective footing, aligning with the meritocracy argument. The Central Department of Organization mandates that all participants in these democratic assessment sessions receive a fact sheet of the cadres' actual work accomplishments before grading these leaders. Table 5 outlines a general guideline for this fact sheet, proposing a set of economic and social indicators to gauge the achievements of local leaders. Local Departments of Organization at all levels have the flexibility to modify these indicators and assign weights based on the specific objectives outlined in their plans submitted annually to the PCs in their jurisdictions. Furthermore, it is required that the relevant statistics supporting these indicators be provided by the functional departments overseeing these fields.

A detailed breakdown of various indicators for Yueyang City is not available on its official website, suggesting that it probably does not assign specific weights in its evaluation of achievements. In fact, this is a common phenomenon among higher levels of government, a point we will return to later. However, some regional governments, particularly at the county level, have followed this guideline more carefully. Table 6 is a form used by Laiwu District in Jinan City, Shandong Province to assess township leaders' achievements in 2017. Some parts are consistent with the meritocratic view. Economic indicators such as "project construction," "attracting businesses and investments," and "fiscal revenues" have the highest individual weights – 100, 100, and 80 out of 1,000, respectively – among thirty-eight categories being measured. Statistics and judgments about their performance are provided by functional departments responsible for these tasks. This ensures some degree of objectivity. However, non-economic indicators are also heavily weighted. Party construction alone is broken down into eleven subcategories and constitutes 23 percent of the total score. Other social development measures, including "farm produce and food quality safety," "precise poverty reduction targeting," and "energy-saving environmental protection," are given high weights. An extra fifty-five points could be added for providing a safer social and living environment for citizens. Moreover, all one-vote-veto (一票否决) items

Table 3 A democratic evaluation form for annual assessment of leading cadres managed by Yueyang City, 2018

Grassroots party-building responsibilities	Poor			
	Fair			
	Fairly good			
	Good			
Integrity	Poor			
	Fair			
	Fairly good			
	Good			
Achievement	Poor			
	Fair			
	Fairly good			
	Good			
Diligence	Poor			
	Fair			
	Fairly good			
	Good			
Ability	Poor			
	Fair			
	Fairly good			
	Good			
Virtue	Poor			
	Fair			
	Fairly good			
	Good			
Overall evaluation	Incompetent			
	Basically competent			
	Competent			
	Excellent			
Current position				
Name				

Note: 1. Please check a mark underneath the item according to your opinion, one mark for each category.

2. No evaluation for non-CCP party member.

Source: Yueyang City Department of Organization official website.

Table 4 Registration form for annual assessment of leading cadres managed by Yueyang City, 2018

Name		Gender		Birth date		Date starting work	
Political outlook		Education		Tenure in current position			
Work unit and position							
Personal summary							

Democratic evaluation	Number of participants	Excellence		Competent		Basically competent		Incompetent		Abstention	
		vote	%	vote	%	vote	%	vote	%	vote	%

Participation in full-time training	
Assessment opinion by the Party Committee	Signature (seal) Year month day
Opinion by the assessed cadre	Signature (seal) Year month day
Opinion by approval organization	Signature (seal) Year month day
Memo	

Note: "Personal summary" should be concise. If needed, attach additional pages.
Source: Yueyang City Department of Organization official website.

concern social developments only, such as family planning, workplace safety, social security, energy conservation, food safety, pollution, farmers' burdens, and fire deaths. Failing in one category results in automatic disqualification of the leading cadre in the assessment, clearly more powerful than the weights of economic indicators.

Supporters of the meritocratic viewpoint might question whether this case represents the entirety of local government assessments in China. It could also signal a shift away from an excessive focus on economic indicators in recent years. Empirically testing this is challenging because not all regional governments quantify cadre achievements, and even fewer disclose their methodologies publicly. Tao, Liu, and Hou (2020) conducted a comprehensive survey of cadre

Table 5 Key elements for analyzing the real work achievement of local party and government leading teams

Categories	Key elements in assessment		Assessment method
Data analysis content concerning annual targets	Economic development	Economic development level	Analysis and assessment should be based on data provided by relevant government departments, in accordance with specific targets set by annual goals
		Comprehensive benefits from economic development	
		Urban–rural residents' income	
		Regional economic development gap	
		Development costs	
	Social development	Basic education	
		Urban employment	
		Health and hygiene	
		Urban–rural cultural lives	
		Public security	
	Sustainable development	Energy-saving, pollution reduction, and environmental protection	
		Ecological construction and protection of farmland and other resources	
		Population and family planning	
		Technological investment and innovation	

Source: Central Department of Organization 2009b.

Table 6 Indictors for assessing township leading teams' achievement in Laiwu District, 2017

Category	Indictors	Weight	Responsible Departments
Transition and development (340)	Project construction	100	Development and Reform Bureau Investment Promotion Bureau
	Attracting businesses and investments	100	Investment Promotion Bureau
	Business environment	30	Industrial and Commerce Association
	Growing key enterprises	20	Business Affair Bureau
	Supporting medium and small enterprises	10	Medium and Small Enterprise Office
Industrial upgrades (130)	Fiscal revenues	80	Finance Bureau
	Industrial zone construction	20	Medium and Small Enterprise Office
	Industrial upgrades	50	Development and Reform Bureau and 9 others
	Farm produce and food quality safety	50	Food and Drug Administration Agriculture Bureau Bureau of Animal Husbandry and Veterinary Medicine
Integral development (40)	Northern city construction	20	Urban Construction Bureau
	Downtown upgrades	–	Urban Construction Bureau Civil Affairs Bureau Comprehensive Administrative Law Enforcement Bureau
	Southern city tourism	–	Tourism Bureau
	Beautiful rural construction	10	Rural Works Office
	Rural sanitary condition	10	Urban Construction Bureau Transportation Bureau Health and Hygiene Office

Category	Item	Value	Bureau
Innovation and development (110)	Reform and innovation	40	Reform Office
	Technological innovation	10	Technology Bureau
			Business Affairs Bureau
	Talent recruitment	40	Department of Organization
	Standardization	20	Market Supervision Bureau
Livelihood protection (150)	Precise poverty reduction targeting	40	Poverty Reduction Office
			Civil Affair Bureau
	Energy-saving environmental protection	40	Environmental Protection Bureau
	Water system environment	10	Water Affairs Bureau
			Environmental Protection Bureau
	Forest and greenery	10	Forest Bureau
	Employment and social security	10	Human Resources and Social Security Bureau
	Civil affairs	10	Civil Affairs Bureau
			Association for Disabled People
	Educational development	10	Education Bureau
	Health services	10	Health and Family Planning Commission
	Culture and sports	10	Culture and Sports Bureau

Table 6 (cont.)

Category	Indictors	Weight	Responsible Departments
Party construction (230)	Party construction	30	Department of Organization
	Party member and team development	20	
	Rural party construction	40	
	Urban community party construction	–	
	Two "news" party construction	20	
	Grassroots united front	10	United Front Department
			Taiwan Affairs Office
			Industrial and Commerce Association
	Party discipline	30	Disciplinary Commission
	Propaganda and ideology work	20	Department of Propaganda
	Social stability maintenance	20	Politics and Law Commission
	Rule of law	10	Justice Bureau
			Legal Affairs Office
	Letters and visits	40	Letters and Visits Bureau
Point addition and deduction	National Civilized City Construction: a maximum addition of 5 points and a deduction of up to 10 points		Propaganda Department
			Safety Supervision Bureau
	Workplace safety, food and drug safety, school and school bus safety, fire safety, and emergency management: a maximum deduction of 10 points each		Food and Drug Administration
			Education Bureau
			Laicheng Public Security Sub-bureau
			Government Emergency Office

One-vote-veto	
Population and family planning	Health and Family Planning Commission
Workplace safety	Safety Supervision Bureau
Comprehensive social security management	Politics and Law Commission
Energy conservation goals	Bureau of Economy and Information Technology
Major food safety incidents	Commerce Bureau
Total reduction of major pollutants	Food and Drug Administration
Alleviating the burden on farmers	Environmental Protection Bureau
Major casualties in large fires	Agriculture Bureau
	Laicheng Public Security Sub-bureau

Source: Laiwu District Party Committee website.

evaluations nationwide in 2006. Hebei Province was among the first to experiment with quantifying cadre evaluations, offering insight into practices before the shift in emphasis. They gathered information on categories and weights used in Cangzhou City. When county-level leading cadres were assessed, twenty-four indicators were used to gauge their performance, with six focusing on economic development and eighteen on social development and party construction. The weight for economic and social/party indicators was split evenly at 50:50, translating to 8.3 percent for each economic indicator and 2.7 percent for each social/party indicator. When assessing township-level leading cadres, nineteen indicators were considered, with 49 percent allocated to economic indicators and 51 percent to social/party indicators. There were fewer one-vote-veto items then, primarily related to birth control, public security, and workplace safety. However, this pattern generally aligned with the trends observed in Laiwu District, Jinan City, in 2017. Notably, economic indicators were never the sole criteria for evaluating leading cadres' achievements.

Advocates of this view might argue that whether economic indicators or others are used, they all gauge a leader's capability to execute tasks deemed crucial by their superiors. Those excelling across these indicators demonstrate higher overall competence. From this perspective, quantifying economic and social/party tasks equally does not necessarily invalidate the notion that cadre assessment aligns with meritocracy. There is a degree of truth in this argument. However, it diverges from the initial meritocracy argument, which asserts that China's cadre assessment system selects and incentivizes officials with strong economic competence, thereby driving the nation's rapid economic growth. It is improbable that excelling in promoting economic development is crucial for establishing party infrastructure in an area. There is a strong reason to suspect that these two tasks require very different personal traits and skill sets. Hence, those ranking high overall might lack the quality for fostering rapid economic growth.

Most important of all, these achievement scores do not directly translate into final merit ratings; they serve as just one component in the entire process. Participants in democratic evaluation sessions reference these scores for assessing the achievement category. Additionally, party leaders overseeing these assessments consider these scores alongside evaluations from democratic sessions to determine final ratings for the leaders being assessed. The party committee's conclusive rating appears on cadres' assessment forms (as in Table 4), alongside merit ratings provided by peers and subordinates, whereas their achievement scores do not. Hence, when Chinese officials refer to cadres' performance rating in the news, it pertains not to their achievement scores but to the subjective judgments of the party committees.

3.2.2 Is Promotion Tied to Assessment?

Another misrepresentation by the meritocratic view lies in the presumed link between cadres' assessment records and their prospects for promotion. It is assumed that higher assessment ratings automatically translate to better promotion chances. However, this is not accurate. Certain clauses in the cadre assessment documents (found in the right column of Table 1) seem to suggest a correlation between cadres' merit ratings and their career paths. For instance, the *Annual Assessment Method for Party and Government Leadership Teams and Cadres (Trial)* of 2009 (Central Department of Organization 2009a) stipulates that cadres with excellent ratings should be commended and encouraged. The 2019 revised version draws closer to linking excellence in assessment to promotion. Cadres who receive an "excellent" rating in assessments will receive rewards, primarily in the form of honors and financial benefits. If a cadre consistently attains an excellent rating for three consecutive years, they might be granted some preference in promotion considerations among other equally qualified candidates. However, this promise remains rather vague and is not corroborated in the Party's formal regulations on the selection and promotion of cadres.

These regulations are outlined in various documents adopted by the Central Committee, which can be found in the left column of Table 1. Within these documents, any mention of this vague promise is absent. Throughout the past forty years, none of these regulations have required cadres to achieve high merit ratings in annual assessments in order for them to qualify for candidacy in promotions. Instead, all promotion candidates must meet some fundamental conditions, such as aligning with socialist ideology, adhering to the Party's foundational guidelines and principles, demonstrating strong revolutionary responsibilities, following the mass line, and upholding democratic centralism. These criteria are notably vague and flexible, subject to interpretation and manipulation by superiors. Stringent qualifications do exist, including minimum tenure at different bureaucratic levels, educational requirements, years in the party, completion of party school training, and good physical health. It may be concluded that the Chinese cadre management system has become more institutionalized, but not in the direction claimed by the proponents of the meritocratic viewpoint.

Conversely, these assessments can have clear negative impacts on a cadre's career prospects. Should a cadre receive fewer than two-thirds of the votes in the "excellent" and "competent" categories during democratic evaluation sessions, the higher Party Committee will conduct remonstration sessions and issue warnings. If more than a third of the voters deem the cadre "incompetent," that cadre may face dismissal or demotion. Similarly, when a cadre is being considered for a higher position, receiving fewer than two-thirds of the votes in the "excellent" and "competent" categories during democratic evaluation sessions automatically disqualifies them as a candidate, precluding their consideration for promotion. It is notable that none of the Central Committee documents mention quantified achievement scores for cadres. What truly holds weight in the promotion process is the voting by the cadre's peers and subordinates, along with the final judgment rendered by the higher-level party committees. Based on the Party's formal rules, a cadre motivated by promotion needs first to secure support from other colleagues and cultivate loyal followers among subordinates, so that no one can use these democratic evaluation sessions to embarrass them and sabotage their political future. This aligns more with the patronage logic.

The contrasting approaches in how the assessment results are used suggests that cadre assessment is more a tool for penalizing underperformers rather than rewarding competent cadres, a point openly acknowledged by the Central Department of Organization. During a press conference introducing the new assessment method, the spokesperson emphasized a critical distinction between investigation (考察) and assessment (考核). Cadre investigation has as its objective to identify qualified cadres for the party, so it tends to focus on cadres' political qualities:

> The assessment of cadres [on the other hand] involves the understanding, verification, and evaluation conducted by the Party Committee (Party Group) and its organizational (personnel) department, based on their cadre management authority. This evaluation covers political qualities, performance capabilities, work effectiveness, and conduct of Party and government leadership teams and leading cadres. It serves as a pivotal basis for strengthening the construction of leadership teams and the cadre workforce. (Central Department of Organization 2019)

The primary goal is to ensure that all cadres remain "on duty and in an active, motivated state." With pressure from annual assessments, cadres are discouraged from holding beliefs such as "smooth sailing after promotion" or "no pressure if not promoted." It is evident that, in the eyes of its designers, the cadre assessment system primarily serves as a means to penalize lackluster performers, encouraging cadres not to evade their responsibilities. Rather than a proactive institutional design aimed at meritocracy, this heavy-handed approach seems to be more appropriately understood as a desperate measure to rectify the shortcomings of the cadre system.

The disconnect between assessments and promotions is well understood in China. In 2013, when the *Regulations on the Selection and Appointment of*

Party and Government Leading Cadres completed its first revision (Central Committee of the CCP 2014), the *People's Daily* invited notable scholars in public administration and party organization to share their thoughts and promote the new regulation. While these researchers praised numerous changes in the cadre selection process, they also highlighted that cadre assessment results should hold greater importance in the promotion of future leaders. Their field experiences revealed a prevalent trend where local governments did not prioritize cadre assessment results, rendering the assessment work a mere formality (流于形式). In fact, even the Central Department of Organization officials admitted that, in their promotion decisions of provincial-level leaders, cadres' assessment results were basically disregarded (Jiang and Luo 2021). The researchers also discovered that many statistics used to evaluate achievements originated from government functional departments under the authority of the reviewed leaders, with no independent verification of their validity (Zhu and Ye 2013). Other scholars have also documented systematic falsification of GDP statistics among Chinese local officials (Chen, Qiao, and Zhu 2021; Wallace 2021). This practice showcases how easily local officials can manipulate the assessment process to avoid unfavorable ratings. It also explains why assessment results cannot be trusted by higher-level party committees for determining promotions. From this angle, the alarmingly high percentage of cadres earning "excellent" or "competent" ratings in the 2021 Gansu Provincial Party Committee's annual assessment cited earlier is no longer surprising. Out of 2,038 leading officials, only 1 percent were deemed unqualified for their positions or for consideration for higher roles – not a very powerful incentive or disincentive.

We lack direct access to cadre merit ratings, making it challenging to observe this disconnect firsthand. However, since 2000, the Central Department of Organization has urged local party committees to publicly disclose the names and basic details of officials slated for promotion. This move aimed to allow public objections to be heard, although not all local governments comply with this directive. Despite this, these disclosures offer some insight into the rationale behind promotions. At the provincial and city levels, the disclosed information typically encompasses the individual's name, gender, party affiliation, previous key roles, current position, and intended new position. In contrast, some county-level disclosures provide more detailed information, presenting their achievements to justify their promotions. For instance, in March 2018, Cangxi County in Guangyuan City, Sichuan Province proposed the promotion of twelve officials, including ten for key township positions. Each official's summary outlined a plethora of major achievements, including various statistics related to agricultural growth, business attraction, poverty eradication, rural development, anti-corruption efforts, and party building, akin to those listed in Table 5. Evidently, the Cangxi Party Committee had conducted assessments of these officials' accomplishments. Among the ten officials selected for township leadership, only one had attained a "class one" merit ranking in one comprehensive assessment during his tenure. Notably, none of the other summaries mentioned their merit ranking in cadre assessment. Since merit ranking was used to justify the promotion of one cadre, it is reasonable to infer that other cadres did not rank highly in their assessments. Among all cadres, township officials are subject to the most quantified and rigorous assessment regulations. If their promotions are not justified on the basis of their final merit rankings, it is hard to imagine merit-based promotion at higher levels.

3.2.3 Is There a Uniform and National System?

Already hinted at in earlier discussions is one more misrepresentation. By relying on the cadre assessment system to explain the fast economic growth in China, the meritocratic viewpoint suggests a national and uniform cadre assessment system throughout the reform period. This does not match the reality either. As Table 1 shows, the first cadre assessment was rolled out for county-level leaders on a trial basis in 1988, and it wasn't until 1998 that an interim regulation aimed to extend this system to all levels of leading cadres was formalized. Even then, the adoption of this system varied widely. The Central Department of Organization did not standardize its implementation across all local departments until later, resulting in significant disparities.

Research by Tao, Liu, and Hou (2020) highlighted substantial differences in national implementation. For instance, Zhejiang and Jiangsu Provincial Party Committees did not apply the cadre assessment system to their city-level leading cadres in 2006. Hebei Provincial Party Committee, on the other hand, stood out as a model of rigorous implementation of central regulations in this regard. In Hebei, city leaders underwent formal assessments based on a set of tasks for their real work achievements, although these tasks were not assigned any specific weights. Moreover, practices at the city level also diverged greatly. For instance, Wenzhou City in Zhejiang Province employed a quantitative assessment for its county leading cadres, whereas Hangzhou City in the same province did not introduce such a system. It wasn't until 2009, when the Central Department of Organization aimed to promote the scientific development ideology, that standardized evaluation forms (e.g. Tables 2 and 5) were suggested to bring greater consistency to cadre evaluation nationwide. But this came after the growth of the Chinese economy had slowed down significantly, undermining any argument attributing China's rapid growth to the cadre evaluation system. It's crucial to highlight that, despite the

Central Department of Organization's efforts, regional governments retained the authority to shape the final formats within their jurisdictions. This allowance has contributed to ongoing regional disparities in compliance that persist to this day.

Amidst the temporal and geographical disparities, there exists a divergence in the extent of implementing task quantification across various government tiers. Proponents of meritocracy argue that the pressure for performance, stemming from the highly centralized hierarchical structure, permeates from the top echelons to the lower tiers of the state apparatus. While quantified tasks are evident at the township levels, as highlighted in both this and preceding sections, the rigorous scientific and quantitative assessments of cadres at the county and city levels are comparatively fewer. Moreover, there's a glaring absence of evidence suggesting such quantification for provincial leaders. Contrary to the proponents' assertion, it appears implausible that provincial leaders, under pressure to fulfill centrally assigned tasks, subject lower tiers to analogous quantitative assessment frameworks. This raises doubts about the purported uniformity in the application of quantitative assessments across different tiers of government and questions the cascading effect of performance pressure from higher to lower levels within the state hierarchy.

When considering the temporal, spatial, and rank heterogeneities, a more intricate image emerges regarding the cadre assessment in post-Mao China. A nationally uniform and highly centralized system has never existed in reality. Instead of functioning as a mechanism to initiate growth-focused competition, and elevate the most capable leaders to higher tiers of the hierarchy, it seems more plausible that the system primarily aims to ensure that the giant and often unruly state apparatus performs its routine functions for the society, as previously explained by an official from the Central Department of Organization. Not surprisingly, grassroots-level cadres bear the most substantial pressures as they directly execute policies and engage with citizens. Even the *People's Daily* criticized local governments for relying on heavy-handed quantitative tasks to execute policies, a sign of administrative laziness. This addiction has resulted in rapid increase in the number of quantified tasks on the assessment sheet (*People's Daily* 2019). This understanding also explains why more affluent regions, not underdeveloped regions as the tournament-competition argument would predict, prioritized economic growth in their cadre assessment. Less-developed regions actually placed more emphasis on non-growth tasks, such as constructing new terraces, restructuring agriculture, birth control, handling farmers' petitions, and managing fiscal transfers from higher authorities – tasks that were immediate and pressing for these local governments (Tao, Liu, and Hou 2020). This distinction in priorities reflects the pragmatic challenges faced by different regions, highlighting a divergence from the presumed singular focus on growth within the cadre assessment system.

3.3 Methodological Challenges

While we demonstrate that no party documents explicitly link cadres' assessments to their promotions up the hierarchical ladder, advocates may still argue that these formal rules are bypassed in reality. Higher party committees exclusively rely on officials' GDP growth records, disregarding other measures and ratings outlined in the formal regulation. This record may be deemed the most objective and visible indicator of an individual's competence. This assertion essentially undermines the formal and institutional basis of the meritocracy argument. It prompts the question of why this circumvention occurs and what political rationales justify this choice by the leaders responsible for personnel appointments. These are important theoretical questions that require thorough and thoughtful examination.

More troubling is the fact that even the purported empirical evidence supporting this association appears quite shaky. For instance, Tao et al. (2010) and Wiebe (2024) have demonstrated that certain findings affirming a positive correlation between GDP growth and promotions are largely driven by data errors and model misspecifications. Upon proper rectification of these issues, GDP growth fails to exhibit any significant impact on cadres' upward mobility. Furthermore, the results regarding the top two leadership positions – number one (party secretary) and number two (governor, mayor, and county magistrate) – are perplexing and inconsistent. As per formal regulations, real work achievements are evaluated for the leadership team within a region, where both top leaders are expected to receive equivalent scores. Although leaders of the government tend to focus more on economic and social developments, party secretaries bear responsibility for the comprehensive development of the region. Interestingly, a common career progression for number two leaders is to ascend to the top position, either within the same region or elsewhere. Therefore, it seems unlikely that they are judged by different criteria. As a result, GDP growth should hold equal weight in the promotion decisions of both leaders, especially when advocates claim that only achievement scores and economic measures are valued in the real world. This claim is corroborated by Li and Zhou's (2005) analysis of provincial party secretaries and governors, where GDP growth has a positive and significant impact on the promotion chances of both provincial party secretaries and governors. In a similar research design, Choi (2012) discovers that higher GDP bolsters the promotion prospects only of party secretaries. Conversely, Chen and Kung (2019) report that governors, rather than party secretaries, are rewarded for faster economic growth. Intriguingly, Choi, Givens, and MacDonald (2021), using the same dataset as their own previous study but incorporating additional years, reveal no positive impact for either party secretaries or governors.

Some of these conflicting outcomes might arise due to variations in the time periods under examination (Sheng 2022). However, responsibility also lies with their methodologies. Almost universally, these studies have relied on panel data incorporating year and region fixed effects (see Table 7). One significant challenge with this kind of model setup is its failure to systematically tackle the identification problem linked to endogeneity, including the matching of officials with specific positions or regions. Even Zhou (2022) concedes that this methodological issue has restricted the advancement of the literature on meritocracy.

This challenge associated with latent variables is illustrated in Figure 1 (Wooldridge 2010). There are two segments that the existing studies have not addressed adequately. As the vertical two-direction arrow indicates, regional officials' economic performance is affected by their patronage networks through financial transfers or preferential policies from their patrons on the top. Similarly, patronage opportunities tend to favor officials with stronger economic outcomes and ample resources. Including both factors is crucial to obtaining unbiased estimates. Many empirical findings regarding meritocracy fail to account for the influence of patronage, resulting in biased estimates for their GDP variables. This issue also affects certain studies that concentrate on the impact of patronage on career advancement.

An even bigger challenge is the circle to the left of the figure. As suggested by Besley, Montalvo, and Reynal-Querol (2011) and Jones and Olken (2005), individual leaders' innate abilities, traits, and values can affect their policy selection and execution. As a result, high-quality people can increase the economic performance of their jurisdictions. This logic should apply to patronage ties as well. High-quality officials, particularly those with strong interpersonal skills or ambition, should have more opportunities to befriend powerful patrons at the top. Since these innate qualities are unobservable, omitting them from regressions can bias the estimates for the economic performance and patronage variables. One solution to this inference problem is to add individual leader fixed effects into the model. For the patronage variable, this in effect exploits the exogeneous network switches caused by the succession of the top leadership because any patronage changes induced by the provincial officials' innate qualities are held constant by the individual fixed effects. Therefore, the coefficient offers a more accurate estimate of the impact of patronage on promotion. For the same reason, this estimation strategy captures the effect of the economic performance variable on promotion when the officials' innate abilities are excluded from the economic outcomes. In a way, models with and without individual fixed effects test somewhat different interpretations of the

Table 7 Existing research on Chinese official promotion

Publications	Locale of the state	Time period	Performance measures	Findings	Patronage ties measures	Findings	Modeling strategies
Shih, Adolph, and Liu 2012	Central Committee	1982–2002	Fiscal revenue growth GDP growth	Zero Zero	Work, hometown, college with GPS	Positive	Cross-sectional with Bayesian inference
Francois, Trebbi, and Xiao 2023	Central Committee	1956–2014			"Shanghai gang" and CCYL gang	Positive	Cross-sectional data with year, hierarchy FEs, and individual controls
Fisman et al. 2020	Central Committee	1956–2017			Hometown and college with Politburo	Negative	Cross-sectional data with work, hometown, college FEs, and individual controls

Study	Patron	Years	Dependent variable	Result	Connection	Result	Method
Li and Zhou 2005	Province #1 and 2	1979–1995	GDP growth	Positive			Panel data with year and province FEs
Tao et al. 2010	Province #1 and 2	1979–2002	GDP growth	Zero			Panel data with year and province FEs
Choi 2012	Province #1 and 2	1989–2009	GDP growth Fiscal revenue growth	Positive for #1 only Positive for #2 only	Work tie with GPSs	Positive for #1 (Jiang's era only)	Multinomial logit
Opper, Nee, and Brehm 2015	Province #1 and 2	1979–2011	GDP growth	Zero	Work, hometown, college with PSC	Positive	Probit with year, office, region FEs
Jia, Kudamatsu, and Seim 2015	Province #1 and 2	1993–2009	GDP growth	Positive for connected officials only	Work, home, college with PSC	Zero	Linear probability model (panel data) with province and year FEs

Table 7 (cont.)

Publications	Locale of the state	Time period	Performance measures	Findings	Patronage ties measures	Findings	Modeling strategies
Choi, Givens, and MacDonald 2021	Province #1 and 2	1989–2018	GDP growth	Zero	Work tie and anecdotal tie with Jiang, Hu, Xi	Positive for Xi only	Panel data (logit) with province FE
Sheng 2022	Province #1 and 2	1978–2018	GDP growth	Positive for Jiang's era only	Work tie with Hu Y., Jiang, Hu J., Xi	Positive for Hu Y. only	Panel data with year, province FEs
Landry, Lü, and Duan 2018	Province, city and county # 1 and 2	1999–2007	Fiscal revenue growth GDP growth	Positive for county #1 and 2 but negative for province #1	Work tie with #1 one level above	Positive for province #1 and county #1	Cross-sectional model with region and year FEs
Chen and Kung 2019	Province and city #1 and 2	2004–2016	GDP growth	Positive for #2 only	Work, home-town, college ties With PSC	Zero	Panel data with year and region FEs

Yao and Zhang 2015	City #1 and 2	1998–2010	Individual residual effects in GDP growth regression	Positive for older leaders only	Provincial work experience	Positive	Panel data with year, province FEs
Zeng and Wong 2021	City and county #1 and 2	1997–2016	GDP growth	Positive			Cross-sectional data with region FEs
Chen and Kung 2016	County #1	1999–2008	GDP growth	Positive	Work, hometown tie with prefecture #1 and #2 CCYL Shanghai gang	Positive	Panel data with county and year FEs

Note: #1=party secretary and #2=governor at the provincial level, mayor at the city level and magistrate at the county level. FEs=fixed effects; GPSs=General Party Secretaries; PSC=Politburo Standing Committee.

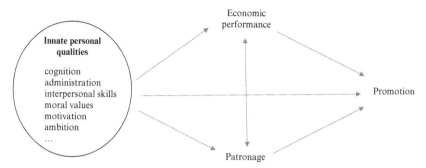

Figure 1 Estimation with a latent variable of personal qualities

meritocracy argument, that is, one with officials' innate qualities and the other with only officials' effort and time-varying local conditions.

3.4 Summary

This section critically evaluates the meritocratic perspective, highlighting critiques that question its suitability in understanding China's post-Mao political economy. A key theoretical challenge emerges as advocates struggle to reconcile a meritocratic system within the context of a one-party political framework. In contrast, the patronage argument, by emphasizing power dynamics, appears more adept at capturing the complexities of Chinese elite politics and offers greater potential as a lens for analyzing the country's political economy. Furthermore, proponents of the meritocratic viewpoint have misrepresented China's cadre management system in multiple dimensions, undermining the factual basis of their perspective. Finally, a methodological challenge facing quantitative studies on elite mobility (including both meritocratic and patronage supporters) underscores the inherent complexities of this analytical approach. Ultimately, while the meritocratic perspective has gained prominence, this section argues for a reassessment, suggesting that the patronage framework might offer a more nuanced understanding of China's intricate political and economic landscape.

4 Provincial Leader Promotion: A Reassessment

We study provincial leaders for a number of reasons. In the post-Mao era, governing a province has become a crucial, if not a necessary, credential for entry into the Politburo, the CCP's executive body. Since Jiang Zemin's era, over 80 percent of Politburo members in every Central Committee have held positions in at least one province before ascending to higher roles, with many having extensive experience across multiple provinces (Huang 2022). Assuming full responsibility over a province gives the officials a good platform to demonstrate their competence, thereby providing a fair test for evaluating the meritocratic viewpoint. Another advantage of utilizing provincial leaders, as opposed to those at lower administrative levels, is data availability. Detailed biographies of provincial leaders are routinely published through official channels and scholarly databases, enabling thorough cross-verification. Conversely, biographical information for officials at city and county levels often suffers from missing data issues, which can compromise statistical analyses. However, beyond the challenge of missing data, the length of available data is a more critical concern for our research. Our identification strategy relies on a long time series dataset to generate more exogenously switched-on network ties. Constructing reliable biography data for city and county officials spanning over twenty years proves exceedingly challenging. We will make an effort to extend our research to these lower tiers in the future, but must limit our empirical evidence to provincial leaders only in this Element.

4.1 Data Sources and Variable Definitions

To construct detailed leader biographies, we have meticulously gathered information from a diverse array of sources. Our research draws from platforms such as people.com.cn (the website of the CCP mouthpiece the *People's Daily*), Baidu Baike (a reputable website containing biographical information on most major political, economic, and social leaders in China, https://baike.baidu.com/), the Chinese Political Elites Database curated by National Chengchi University (https://cped.nccu.edu.tw/), and databases maintained by fellow researchers. When confronted with conflicting information, our preference leans toward entries sourced from government official websites, prioritizing official records for accuracy and reliability. Moreover, in the case of princeling designations, we go beyond conventional sources, referring to autobiographies and memoirs authored by the leaders themselves and their family members whenever available. Our commitment to cross-referencing multiple sources, including official records and familial accounts, ensures a comprehensive and accurate compilation of leader biographies.

The final database comprises all provincial party secretaries and governors spanning the period from 1978 to 2020. Our regression analysis is largely drawn on a balanced three-dimensional panel dataset, distinguishing observations by year, province, and position (party secretary or governor). In addition to basic demographic details such as age, gender, ethnicity, education, and birthplace, our dataset offers exhaustive information about their career trajectories.

We track their journey from initial job assignments or colleges until retirement for former leaders or their current offices by July 1, 2021.

Promotion. The primary dependent variable focuses on elite mobility. We adopt a widely accepted definition from existing literature and treat it as a dichotomous variable. For provincial party secretaries, a move is coded 1 if the official ascends to a national leadership position, as outlined in Table 8. In the case of governors, promotions further include transitions to provincial party secretaries and ministers within the central government. Any other forms of turnover are coded 0. This coding strategy allows us to narrow our focus to factors influencing promotions, disentangling the complexities surrounding various career changes, notably distinguishing between normal retirement and

Table 8 Definition of promotion

	New position	Promotion	Strict promotion
Provincial Party Secretary	Members of the PSC, Politburo Members, Premier, Vice-Premier, State Councilors	Yes	Yes
	NPC and NPPCC* chairman, vice-chairman	Yes	No
	Central Party Secretariat	Yes	Yes
	Prosecutor-General of the Supreme People's Procuratorate	Yes	Yes
	President of the Supreme People's Court	Yes	Yes
Provincial Governor	Members of the PSC, Politburo Members, Premier, Vice-Premier, State Councilors	Yes	Yes
	NPC and NPPCC chairman, vice-chairman	Yes	No
	Central Party Secretariat	Yes	Yes
	Prosecutor-General of the Supreme People's Procuratorate	Yes	Yes
	President of the Supreme People's Court	Yes	Yes
	Provincial Party Secretary	Yes	Yes
	Ministers, Commissioners and Vice Minister of NDRC	Yes	Yes

Note: NPPCC=National People's Political Consultative Conference; NDRC=National Development and Reform Commission.

demotion. However, debates may arise regarding the political status of NPC (National People's Congress) and CPPCC (Chinese People's Political Consultative Conference), with some researchers arguing that these positions are reserved for semi-retired officials and, thus, their political power cannot be equated with other branches at the top. To address this contention, we refine our definition by adding a stricter definition and excluding these positions from promotions. We conduct all regressions in the robustness section (Section 4.4) to examine the impact of this adjustment on our analysis.[2]

Figure 2 illustrates the percentage of provincial officials receiving promotions over the specified time span. As expected, the big spikes coincide with the Party's quinquennial meetings. However, what stands out is the notable frequency of promotions to the central top during non-Party Congress years. For instance, in 1994, a year without a Party Congress, approximately 13 percent of provincial leaders ascended to the top echelon, compared to about 16 percent during the Party

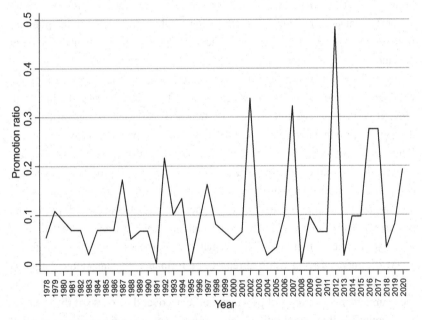

Figure 2 Provincial official promotion ratio by year, 1978–2020

---

[2] All these definitions are based on official rankings in the hierarchy. In practice, officials with equal bureaucratic rankings may control varying levels of resource and command different levels of prestige and power within the political system. One alternative method is to further differentiate equally ranked leaders based on the geographical, economic, and population size of their jurisdictions. This approach should add more nuance and realism to the promotion variable, but the selection of appropriate weights may rely on researchers' subjective judgment.

Congress year of 1997. Similarly, the same share of provincial leaders was promoted in 2016 and 2017, despite the former falling outside the formal term cycle defined by the Party Congress. This dynamic suggests a cadre management system that appears less institutionalized, despite efforts to standardize career assessment and promotion processes. The decision-making regarding personnel often occurs without formal oversight or checks from the Party's highest body.

Performance. A meritocratic state aims to select competent officials, yet measuring competence is complex. It encompasses various facets such as cognitive ability, administrative aptitude, leadership style, interpersonal skills, and personal values. These inherent qualities significantly impact how individuals execute tasks, but quantifying them as a single concept poses challenges. In the context of assessing competence, the tournament-competition literature has simplified this complexity by using quantitative targets established by the Department of Organization as proxies. Notably, among Chinese officials and policy analysts, GDP growth stands as a crucial "hard indicator" for evaluating the performance of local governments. This emphasis is evident in the publication of growth rate statistics for all levels of local governments, spanning provinces, cities, and counties – an uncommon practice globally.[3]

Naturally, in most empirical studies researchers have focused on the regional GDP growth rate as the primary proxy for official competence. In line with previous literature, we follow this practice and use the GDP growth rate to measure a provincial leader's performance and competence. Provincial GDP figures are sourced from the National Bureau of Statistics website (www.stats.gov.cn/sj/) and real GDP growth rates are calculated for all provinces. To ensure compatibility across varying macroeconomic conditions and time frames, we standardize these figures. Firstly, we subtract annual national growth rates from provincial figures. Then, we divide the residuals by the standard deviation of regional growth for that year. This normalization process essentially transforms all GDP figures into a measure of relative performance. Certain studies suggests that the Department of Organization adopts a long-term perspective and examines the aggregate performance of provincial officials over the course of their tenure. To account for this possibility, we further calculate a moving average of GDP growth rates. This calculation starts with the official's appointment and changes as their tenure progresses. By considering a moving average, any single year's performance fluctuations, driven by unique factors, are smoothed out, allowing us to capture a more enduring evaluation of official competence.

---

[3] Some researchers have used other criteria, such as pollution control or social stability, to measure leaders' performance. Since our main concern is economic development as assumed in the tournament literature, we follow the mainstream measure of GDP growth rate.

Patronage networks. Our primary measure of patronage networks focuses on officials' personal connections established through prior collaborations with the top leaders in their previous roles. It is widely acknowledged that, following Mao's passing, Deng, Jiang, Hu, and Xi represent the leadership cores of the party in their respective generations. These leaders possess both the necessity and the authority to promote select provincial officials to the national level, ensuring their political control and facilitating the implementation of favored policies nationwide. In our database, we identify all leaders' work experiences, detailing dates, regions, organizations, and positions held. Utilizing computer programs, we locate all dyads between provincial leaders and the leadership cores with shared regional and organizational identifiers during the same time frame. To refine these ties, we eliminate pairs with time overlaps of less than one year or rank differences exceeding two. Such pairs are less likely to have had sufficient time and opportunities to cultivate strong connections. Additionally, manual checks are conducted to verify the accuracy of these identified ties. Previous studies have highlighted additional personal ties maintained through shared birthplaces and colleges, such as the well-known "Shanxi Gang" and "Tsinghua Gang" in recent years. Birthplace ties and college ties are coded 1 if the provincial leader shares the same birth province or university as their contemporary core leader.

Among empirical researchers on elite politics, there is a debate regarding the efficacy of utilizing work overlap as a measure of patronage connections. Keller (2016) adeptly summarizes this discussion and advocates for the value of work ties in studying patronage politics. An alternative method involves coding patronage ties to leadership pairs only if the client is appointed by the patron during their period of overlap. However, this approach has several limitations. Firstly, not all patronage ties align with formal personnel authorities. The CCP's cadre management system operates on a one-level-down basis, where a leader holds formal authority over appointments only one administrative level below. Yet, patrons often exert informal influence over other members within the same hierarchical tier. For instance, the secretary-general of the Party Committee and the head of the Department of Organization, both members of the Party's Standing Committee at various levels, are typically among the closest clients of the party secretary. While the appointments of these officials are determined by party committees one level higher, the party secretary often wields informal influence and selects trusted allies for these crucial positions. Such ties would be overlooked by the alternative method but are captured by our approach.

Secondly, following the same logic, the existence of informal influence also suggests that officials one level down might be appointed by the regional party secretaries but might not necessarily be their close allies. Insights gleaned from numerous interviews with government officials, particularly those associated with the Department of Organization, indicate that the control of personnel one level down is frequently influenced by informal forces stemming from competing factions at higher levels within the Party. Yan's (2017) personal account sheds light on the CCP's frequent consultations with party elders for personnel arrangements in regional governments, leveraging their informal networks, as observed in Bo Yibo's influence over Shanxi. Francois, Trebbi, and Xiao (2023) also demonstrate that leadership lineups at all levels often reflect factional power dynamics at the top. Given these intricate dynamics, employing a formal mechanism to measure informal ties seems unsuitable.

Thirdly, by labeling all subordinates appointed under the patron's tenure as having patronage ties, this supposedly restrictive method in fact inflates the measure too broadly. Our definition of patronage shows that about 32 percent of provincial leaders have any work ties with the members of the PSC. Landry, Lü, and Duan (2018) use the "restrictive" definition but suggest much higher percentages, with 55 percent of provincial party secretaries and 39 percent of provincial governors having work ties with the PSC. This discrepancy indicates that the "restrictive" definition does not effectively filter out what it claims to be unreal ties. A key factor contributing to this discrepancy is how current leadership lineups are treated. In our definition, only work ties established before the patron and the client assumed their current positions are considered as patronage ties. In contrast, other studies code all current subordinates as having patronage ties with the party secretaries or members of the PSC as long as their appointments are made under the latter's tenure. As criticized already, this is not a reasonable approach to Chinese highly informal personnel politics. By this measure, toward the end of the patrons' terms, almost all subordinates are deemed to have patronage ties with their superiors. This contradicts our understanding of patronage politics in China.

Finally, from a methodological standpoint, our approach does not significantly affect our inferences. Our work tie measure effectively captures the informal and frequent personal interactions among these leaders. Leadership pairs commonly recurring in our patronage category involve party/government leading cadres and their personal secretaries. While these ties align with our understanding of patronage, our approach might categorize certain leadership pairs as "patronage" even without establishing a genuine bond beyond their collaborative work experience. However, this shouldn't pose a significant issue. If an indicator, despite some false positive cases due to the less restrictive definition, still indicates a positive impact of patronage, it underscores the genuine influence of patronage, possibly being even more substantial than our estimation. Hence, any introduced bias would actually work against our hypothesized relationship. It may not be ideal, but it could be more reliable than the alternative coding method since we can anticipate the direction of the bias.

Table 9 summarizes these patronage ties in our sample. Throughout the entire period, about 10 percent of provincial officials enjoyed work ties with their contemporary core leaders. Provincial party secretaries were almost twice as likely to be connected than the governors. Conversely, patronage ties through university and birthplace were less common. Debates persist regarding whether the leadership core alone has total control over personnel decisions at the top. Some scholars believe that the PSC holds collective decision-making power in this regard. Therefore, patronage ties with these leaders could also influence promotion chances. For robustness tests, we define patronage ties differently, encompassing provincial officials' connections with the General Party Secretary and members of the PSC.

Table 9 Descriptive statistics of patronage networks

	Full sample	Secretary	Governor
With current core leaders			
Work tie	0.102	0.125	0.078
	(0.302)	(0.331)	(0.269)
College tie	0.017	0.013	0.022
	(0.130)	(0.112)	(0.146)
Birthplace tie	0.070	0.084	0.056
	(0.255)	(0.278)	(0.229)
With current GPSs			
Work tie	0.096	0.122	0.070
	(0.294)	(0.327)	(0.255)
College tie	0.017	0.013	0.022
	(0.130)	(0.112)	(0.146)
Birthplace tie	0.072	0.083	0.060
	(0.258)	(0.276)	(0.238)
With all current PSC members			
Work tie	0.324	0.371	0.277
	(0.468)	(0.483)	(0.448)
College tie	0.084	0.084	0.084
	(0.278)	(0.278)	(0.278)
Birthplace tie	0.309	0.341	0.276
	(0.462)	(0.474)	(0.447)
Observations	2,599	1,302	1,297

Note: GPSs=General Party Secretaries; PSC= Politburo Standing Committee.

According to scholars specializing in Chinese patronage politics, the CCYL and the princelings represent two influential informal groups in post-Mao elite politics. We adhere to the methodology established by these researchers and designate CCYL central as 1 if a provincial leader possesses work experience in the CCYL central offices. Similarly, princeling is marked 1 if the leader has a "red gene" within their family. To ensure accuracy in identifying family lineages, we exercise extreme caution, relying solely on official sources such as government websites, documents, and autobiographies. Whenever contradictory information arises from multiple sources, we omit the princeling designation for the provincial leader. Unlike the three personal ties (work tie, birthplace tie, and college tie), CCYL central and princeling do not measure dyadic relationships between a provincial official and their contemporary core leader. Instead, they gauge provincial leaders' affiliation with these two informal groups. These affiliations, characterized by certain commonalities (e.g., the representation of young idealists for CCYL central and revolutionary lineage for princeling), likely foster cohesion among group members, facilitating trust-building and the exchange of patronage within these circles. It is plausible that these variables capture some enduring yet less overt networking within the Party, such as the sustained influence of retired "old revolutionaries." However, lacking direct links to the incumbent top leadership, these network ties do not activate or deactivate with changes in the party leadership. Consequently, our identification strategy, as will be outlined in Section 4.2, may not resolve the potential endogenous issue for these two variables. Therefore, the results should be interpreted with some caution.

Table 10 summarizes major variables included in our regression analyses. There is some indication that patronage has influenced the promotion of provincial leaders. Within our sample, approximately 10 percent of provincial leaders receive promotions. However, this figure increases to 16.7 percent for officials with patronage ties, contrasting with 10.0 percent for unconnected officials – an increase of 67 percent. This advantage holds true even with a stricter definition of promotion. Further suggestive evidence can be found in the educational background of differently connected officials. On average, 57.1 percent of provincial leaders possess formal university-level education. This percentage drops to 43.7 percent for officials with patronage ties. It is hard to definitively equate formal education with a person's competence, but being admitted to universities does offer some measure of leaders' overall qualities. From this perspective, more competent officials seem to have been shunned by patrons – a trade-off previously discussed. In the following section, we delve into more rigorous methods to thoroughly investigate whether these initial findings can withstand more detailed scrutiny.

Table 10 Descriptive statistics

	Full sample	Connected	Unconnected	Secretary	Governor
Promotion					
Promotion	0.107	0.167	0.100	0.0668	0.147
	(0.309)	(0.374)	(0.300)	(0.250)	(0.355)
Strict	0.0973	0.156	0.0908	0.0576	0.137
promotion	(0.296)	(0.363)	(0.287)	(0.233)	(0.344)
Performance					
Annual growth	10.21	9.933	10.24	10.21	10.20
rate	(4.237)	(4.946)	(4.149)	(4.233)	(4.242)
Moving	−0.012	−0.015	−0.012	−0.009	−0.015
average of	(0.599)	(0.719)	(0.584)	(0.569)	(0.628)
normalized					
growth rate					
Other ties					
Princeling	0.0369	0.0266	0.0381	0.0353	0.0386
	(0.189)	(0.161)	(0.191)	(0.185)	(0.193)
CCYL central	0.0685	0.194	0.0544	0.0806	0.0563
	(0.253)	(0.396)	(0.227)	(0.272)	(0.231)
Individual					
controls					
Age	59.58	60.46	59.48	60.67	58.49
	(4.877)	(5.306)	(4.818)	(4.607)	(4.899)
Gender	0.985	1	0.983	0.993	0.977
	(0.122)	(0)	(0.128)	(0.0829)	(0.150)
Ethnicity	0.886	0.875	0.887	0.973	0.799
	(0.318)	(0.332)	(0.316)	(0.162)	(0.401)
Formal	0.558	0.437	0.571	0.508	0.608
education	(0.497)	(0.497)	(0.495)	(0.500)	(0.488)
(college and					
above)					
Position	0.501	0.608	0.489	1.000	0.000
	(0.500)	(0.489)	(0.500)	(0.000)	(0.000)
Tenure length	3.144	2.643	3.200	3.306	2.981
	(2.092)	(1.654)	(2.129)	(2.205)	(1.960)
Observations	2,599	263	2,336	1,302	1,297

4.2 Baseline Model and Results

We estimate the following linear probability model:

$$Promotion_{i,o,p,t+1} = \alpha G_{iopt} + \beta Patronage_{it} + x'_{it}\rho + \mu_p + \sigma_t + \theta_i + \varepsilon_{iopt} \quad (1)$$

where $Promotion_{i,o,p,t+1}$ is the promotion variable for provincial leader i in office o (governor or secretary) of province p in year $t+1$. Then, G_{iopt} is the moving average of normalized growth rate of province p from the year leader i assumes office o to year t. $Patronage_{it}$ is leader i's network tie status in year t. These two are key independent variables used to test the meritocracy and patronage hypotheses. Further, X_{it} is a vector of standard individual covariates, including both time-invariant demographics – *gender, college education, ethnicity* – and time-varying factors – *age, position* (party secretary=1), *years in office* (a set of dummies indicating years two to twelve).[4] Previous studies have suggested that these personal demographics and position-related factors can affect a leader's chance of upward mobility.

There are also regional and temporal variations in official mobility. For instance, Figure 3 demonstrates that a remarkable 68 percent of party secretaries

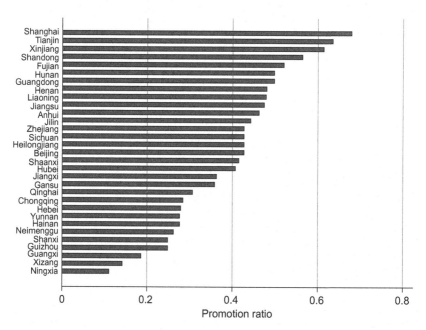

Figure 3 Upward mobility of provincial-level leaders by region

---

and mayors in Shanghai were promoted between 1978 and 2020, while in Ningxia that number was only 11 percent. Similarly, official promotion is more likely before the quinquennial Party Congress and People's Congress when all officials reach their formal five-year terms and need to be reappointed (Figure 2). Respectively, μ_p and σ_t represent provincial fixed effects and year fixed effects. Standard errors are clustered at the province level due to the likely serial correlation within each province regarding growth rates and error terms. Finally, a set of provincial leader fixed effects θ_i is introduced to absorb unobserved individual specific heterogeneities that correlate with patronage networks and GDP growth. As discussed in the methodological segment in Section 3.3, these individual fixed effects can mitigate identification problems present in prior empirical studies.

Table 11 presents the baseline results concerning the impact of performance and patronage on provincial official promotions. We begin with a straightforward model that incorporates solely the performance measure and other controls, excluding the patronage variables and individual fixed effects – this aligns with the conventional choice among scholars advocating for the meritocracy argument. The coefficient associated with the growth rate variable is negative but lacks statistical significance at conventional levels. In contrast to prior studies, our regression does not support the meritocracy hypothesis despite a similar model specification. Patronage variables are introduced in Model 2. It demonstrates that patronage ties established through work connections with the core leader yield a positive and statistically highly significant impact on an official's upward mobility. Holding other factors constant, connected provincial officials exhibit a 7 percent higher probability of promotion compared with their unconnected peers. Given that the average promotion rate in our dataset is around 10 percent, this manifests as a 75 percent increase attributable to these patronage ties. Notably, the coefficients associated with college ties and birthplace ties with the core are statistically indistinguishable from zero across all models. Neither princeling nor CCYL central significantly impacts officials' chances of promotion, despite both coefficients displaying positivity.

However, these estimates are subject to bias due to the exclusion of unobserved personal quality variables. Models 3 and 4 in Table 11 substitute time-invariant individual control variables with a series of individual fixed effects specific to provincial officials while maintaining other specifications. Notably, due to their time-invariant nature for each individual, the variables related to princeling and CCYL central are excluded from these regressions. All coefficients are in general agreement with those in the first two columns, but some subtle yet important theoretical distinctions emerge. Firstly, the coefficient of the growth rate assumes different connotations concerning official performance. In Models 1–2, economic

Table 11 Explaining provincial official promotion, 1978–2020

	1=Promoted at $t+1$		Within-person effects	
	(1)	**(2)**	**(3)**	**(4)**
Performance				
Growth rate	−0.003	−0.003	−0.004	−0.005
	(0.009)	(0.009)	(0.017)	(0.017)
Patronage networks				
Work tie with the current core		0.075***		0.175**
		(0.021)		(0.066)
College tie with the current core		−0.003		0.031
		(0.035)		(0.089)
Birthplace tie with the current core		0.010		0.003
		(0.025)		(0.032)
Princeling		0.053		
		(0.040)		
CCYL central		0.022		
		(0.024)		
Time-variant individual controls	Yes	Yes	Yes	Yes
Time-invariant individual controls	Yes	Yes	No	No
Individual FEs	No	No	Yes	Yes
Year FEs	Yes	Yes	Yes	Yes
Province FEs	Yes	Yes	Yes	Yes
Observations	2,597	2,597	2,583	2,583

Note: Growth rate is the moving average of normalized growth rate since assuming office. Time-invariant individual controls are *gender, college education, ethnicity* and time-variant individual controls are *age, position* (party secretary=1 and governor=0), *years in office* (a set of dummies indicating years two to twelve). Only coefficients of key independent variables are reported. FEs=fixed effects.
*** p<0.01, ** p<0.05, * p<0.1. Robust standard errors are clustered at the provincial level in parentheses.

growth partly incorporates the influence of provincial leaders' personal qualities, where higher growth potentially signifies greater merit. However, in Models 3–4 with individual fixed effects, higher economic growth rates stem from factors beyond innate individual qualities, encompassing leaders' efforts, time-varying local industrial and resource endowments, or even sheer luck. Since the tournament-competition hypothesis may be interpreted either way, depending on the particular emphasis of the researcher, the results from these models together present a more robust empirical foundation for challenging the meritocracy hypothesis. Notably, higher economic growth rates actually decrease, rather than increase, the likelihood of promotion for provincial leaders.

Secondly, the inclusion of individual fixed effects in Models 3–4 refines the interpretation of the coefficients related to work ties. This adjustment offers a clearer understanding of the effect of patronage on promotion, thereby bolstering the validity of the patronage hypothesis. Remarkably, these coefficients more than double that in Model 2. Holding all else constant, provincial officials with work ties to core leaders increase (or decrease) their chances of promotion by an additional 17 percentage points when these ties are activated (or severed) due to the exogenous change of the core leader at the helm. Given the mere 10 percent average promotion rate within our dataset, the substantial underestimation of the patronage effect in the initial four models is notably significant. As Model 2 partially absorbs the impact of personal qualities, it is plausible to infer that highly capable provincial officials might actually encounter resistance from potential patrons. While this effect cannot be observed directly, it aligns with the theoretical prediction by Egorov and Sonin (2011): high-quality officials, possessing more appealing options from potential rivals, might consequently be viewed as less reliable. If personal qualities are proxied by college education, our data indicates that 57 percent of unconnected officials hold college degrees, while only 44 percent of connected officials do, as discussed earlier. However, this piece of evidence serves as a suggestive observation only and needs to be empirically verified through different research designs.

4.3 Extension Analysis

The preceding results illustrate the broad trends in post-Mao China and underscore the systemic inclination toward patronage. However, it is plausible that individual core leaders, confronting varied political environments, might prioritize the promotion of trustworthy yet less-capable followers differently. To delve deeper, we segment our data into four distinct core leadership periods and conduct separate runs of the baseline model. The outcomes are outlined in Table 12. However, a word of caution precedes our analysis: given the absence of top-down exogenous changes within each period, we are unable to introduce officials' individual fixed effects to estimate a clearer coefficient for the patronage variables. Hence, these results, albeit supportive of our observations, should be approached with caution.

Table 12 Heterogeneity in provincial official promotion, 1978–2020

	Deng era		Jiang era		Hu era		Xi era	
	(1)	(2)	(3)	(4)	(5)	(6)	(7)	(8)
Performance								
Growth rate	−0.007	−0.007	−0.057	−0.052	0.013	0.017	0.019	0.018
	(0.011)	(0.011)	(0.037)	(0.038)	(0.032)	(0.032)	(0.033)	(0.032)
Patronage networks								
Work tie with the current core		0.028		0.125*		0.091**		0.112**
		(0.039)		(0.062)		(0.043)		(0.049)
College tie with the current core		—		−0.058		0.098		−0.166**
				(0.076)		(0.100)		(0.065)
Birthplace tie with the current core		−0.022		−0.059		0.058		0.092
		(0.038)		(0.044)		(0.044)		(0.079)
Princeling	0.092	0.094	−0.001	−0.026	0.083	0.077	−0.035	−0.040
	(0.068)	(0.067)	(0.092)	(0.096)	(0.054)	(0.050)	(0.081)	(0.096)
CCYL central	0.067**	0.067**	−0.272***	−0.272***	0.040	−0.011	0.042	0.007
	(0.031)	(0.030)	(0.053)	(0.059)	(0.035)	(0.042)	(0.059)	(0.063)
Time-variant individual controls	Yes	Yes	Yes	Yes	Yes	Yes	Yes	Yes
Time-invariant individual controls	Yes	No	Yes	No	Yes	No	Yes	No

Individual FEs	No	Yes	No	Yes	No	Yes	No	Yes
Year FEs	Yes	Yes	Yes	Yes	Yes	Yes	Yes	Yes
Province FEs	Yes	Yes	Yes	Yes	Yes	Yes	Yes	Yes
Observations	869	869	612	612	615	615	496	496

Note: Growth rate is the moving average of normalized growth rate since assuming office. Time-invariant individual controls are *gender, college education, ethnicity* and time-variant individual controls are *age, position* (party secretary=1 and governor=0), *years in office* (a set of dummies indicating year two to twelve). Only coefficients of key independent variables are reported. The coefficient of college tie is omitted during the Deng era because of collinearity. FEs=fixed effects.

*** p<0.01, ** p<0.05, * p<0.1. Robust standard errors are clustered at the provincial level in parentheses.

There exist heterogeneities within both performance and patronage variables across different eras. Across all periods, the coefficient depicting the relationship between economic growth and promotion is statistically indistinguishable from zero. However, the coefficient for the Jiang era is getting close to the conventional level of statistical significance, even though its negative sign suggests that high performance actually reduces the leader's chance of promotion. This is the opposite of the meritocratic argument. Notably, Jiang's legacy includes promoting numerous officials from his Shanghai base, as evidenced by the substantial coefficient associated with work ties. This era also saw economic restructuring in state-owned enterprises, resulting in slower growth rates in more developed regions throughout the 1990s. Moreover, the Western Development Strategy propelled some underdeveloped regions, like Inner Mongolia and Chongqing, to the forefront of economic growth in the country. But leaders in these regions rarely had a chance to be promoted to the center.

The coefficient related to work ties remains predominantly positive and statistically significant, mirroring the magnitudes observed in Table 11. The Deng era presents a unique scenario: to consolidate power from Maoists, Deng relied on trustworthy followers from his earlier revolutionary years in provincial power struggles. Subsequently, as these battles concluded, Deng effectively persuaded these aged followers into semi-retirement by establishing the Consultative Committee of the Party (顾问委员会). This partly explains the smaller, positive, but statistically insignificant coefficient for the work tie variable. Another notable finding is the significant impact of CCYL central during the Deng and Jiang eras. Deng, aiming to transfer power to younger and more educated leaders, handpicked Hu Jintao as Jiang's successor and facilitated the rise of cadres associated with CCYL. This strategic move was evidently aimed at curbing the power ambition of Jiang. Naturally, Jiang did not take this very well and, upon assuming power, aggressively promoted leaders from his Shanghai base and people within his close personal circles, while sidelining cadres with CCYL affiliations. The same succession dynamics at the top can explain the negative and statistically significant coefficient of college ties for Xi. His predecessor, Hu Jintao, was also a graduate of Tsinghua University. Therefore, most Tsinghua graduates among provincial leaders in the early years of Xi's rule were probably tied with Hu Jintao. Xi needed to cleanse these people and replaced them with his trusted followers from Fujian and Zhejiang.

These results largely align with the primary findings from the baseline model in terms of the main impacts of performance and patronage, but offer a more nuanced picture of power transition in post-Mao China. However, due to the inability to incorporate individual fixed effects, these estimates provide only suggestive evidence and warrant cautious interpretation.

4.4 Robustness

We conduct a series of robustness checks on our baseline results. Initially, some may question our definition of core leaders. Despite Deng's de facto rule in the 1980s, Hu Yaobang and Zhao Ziyang formally held the Party's title of General Party Secretary. In the first two columns of Table 13, we employ personal ties with the GPS as a measure of patronage networks, keeping other variables and model specifications unchanged. Encouragingly, the outcomes align closely with those of the baseline model. Like Table 11, these findings reject the meritocratic hypothesis, indicating that only work ties with the GPS can augment a provincial official's chances of further promotion. Similar to the earlier

Table 13 Networks measured by ties with the GPS and all PSC members, 1978–2020

	1=Promoted at $t+1$			
	With current GPSs		With all current PSC members	
		Within-person effects		Within-person effects
	(1)	(2)	(3)	(4)
Performance				
Growth rate	−0.003	−0.006	−0.002	−0.002
	(0.008)	(0.017)	(0.008)	(0.016)
Patronage networks				
Work tie	0.082***	0.144***	0.040**	0.089*
	(0.021)	(0.041)	(0.013)	(0.046)
College tie	0.019	0.153	0.041	0.230**
	(0.039)	(0.186)	(0.028)	(0.094)
Birthplace tie	−0.005	0.014	0.011	0.043*
	(0.040)	(0.029)	(0.010)	(0.025)
Princeling	0.052		0.049	
	(0.040)		(0.040)	
CCYL central	0.010		0.018	
	(0.024)		(0.022)	

Table 13 (cont.)

	1=Promoted at *t+1*			
Time-variant individual controls	Yes	Yes	Yes	Yes
Time-invariant individual controls	Yes	No	Yes	No
Individual FEs	No	Yes	No	Yes
Year FEs	Yes	Yes	Yes	Yes
Province FEs	Yes	Yes	Yes	Yes
Observations	2,597	2,583	2,597	2,583

Note: Growth rate is the moving average of normalized growth rate since assuming office. Time-invariant individual controls are *gender, college education, ethnicity*. And time-variant individual controls are *age, position* (party secretary=1 and governor=0), *years-in-office* (a set of dummies indicating years two to twelve). Only coefficients of key independent variables are reported. FEs=fixed effects; GPSs=General Party Secretaries; PSC=Politburo Standing Committee.
*** $p<0.01$, ** $p<0.05$, * $p<0.1$. Robust standard errors are clustered at the provincial level in parentheses.

result in the baseline model, the coefficient associated with work ties almost doubles upon inclusion of officials' individual fixed effects.

Some analysts of Chinese elite politics believe that the CCP has followed the principle of collective leadership during the post-Mao era. They propose that decision-making power regarding personnel is dispersed among a handful of influential figures, typically representing the interests of competing factions. Building on these studies, we utilize personal ties with all members of the PSC as a measure of patronage networks. Columns 3 and 4 of Table 13 use these personal ties and the results largely remain consistent concerning the two competing hypotheses. Compared with the core leaders, the effect of patronage for other PSC members is smaller; therefore there is a drop in the coefficient. Considering the supersized power of the leadership core within the Communist Party, this decline is expected. The only noticeable change is that the coefficients of *college tie* and *birthplace tie* with all PSC members become statistically significant at conventional levels. This suggests that, even though the core leaders may favor provincial officials with work ties, other PSC members seem to promote followers from their college circles and birthplace circles.

Another potential query could arise regarding our definition of promotion. We have considered assuming chairman and vice-chairman positions in the NPC and the CPPCC as promotions for provincial leaders. These positions are regarded as national-level positions according to the bureaucratic ranking system. However, there might be an argument that these roles lack substantial power and are reserved for leaders soon to retire from the power center. In Table 14, we redefine promotion by excluding these ceremonial positions and rerun all previous models. The results remain remarkably consistent with those in earlier Tables.

4.5 Summary

Provincial leaders hold a significant position within Chinese politics, and their advancement to higher echelons is heavily influenced by their personal ties with top leaders. This upward mobility is crucial for patrons to secure political support and financial backing, ensuring their survival in the complex political landscape. Each faction's need to maintain a consistent flow of members into influential positions is imperative for safeguarding its interests in the policy-making process. However, the prevalent evidence doesn't support the notion of meritocratic promotions. Despite various metrics being used to gauge economic performance, such as annual or term-based assessments and whether personal efforts and luck are considered, higher GDP growth rates do not bolster the chances of provincial leaders' promotions.

Advocates of the meritocratic stance have argued that, even though provincial-level promotion may be dominated by personal ties and nepotism, lower-level leaders are being systematically evaluated based on merit, and outstanding performance is crucial for their promotion. Manion (2023) has carried out a thorough survey of major empirical studies of the meritocratic argument and noticed similar inconsistency. Instead of calling into question this line of argument, she seems to accept some analysts' *ex post* rationalization of a dichotomous cadre system in China, where patronage rules the top and meritocracy operates at the grassroots level. Segregating the whole cadre system into two distinctive realms offers an easy way out of the inconvenient empirical findings but, in our view, it does not align well with the reality. These researchers essentially assume that only national leaders at the very top are concerned about political survival. As we discussed in Section 3, this view overlooks the fact that the Chinese cadre system is highly decentralized. Leaders at grassroots levels face similar political imperatives as their higher counterparts. In order to survive, they must rely on trusted clients and allies to provide political support and financial resources. In his ethnographic studies of a central Chinese county, Feng (2010) offers fascinating details about how county elites manipulated the cadre assessment system to weaken its effectiveness. Moreover, local elites have intricately woven dense patronage networks,

Table 14 Promotion measured by narrower definitions, 1978–2020

	1=Promoted at *t+1*					
	With current core		With current GPSs		With all current PSC members	
		Within-person effects		Within-person effects		Within-person effects
	(1)	(2)	(3)	(4)	(5)	(6)
Performance						
Growth rate	−0.002	−0.004	−0.002	−0.005	−0.001	−0.000
	(0.009)	(0.016)	(0.009)	(0.016)	(0.009)	(0.016)
Patronage networks						
Work tie	0.064***	0.171**	0.076***	0.143***	0.035**	0.088*
	(0.019)	(0.066)	(0.022)	(0.043)	(0.013)	(0.047)
College tie	−0.008	0.060	0.014	0.179	0.044	0.250**
	(0.036)	(0.102)	(0.052)	(0.194)	(0.029)	(0.094)
Birthplace tie	0.016	−0.004	0.002	0.003	0.018*	0.047*
	(0.023)	(0.031)	(0.020)	(0.028)	(0.011)	(0.024)
Princeling	0.050		0.049		0.046	
	(0.041)		(0.041)		(0.041)	
CCYL central	0.025		0.013		0.021	
	(0.023)		(0.024)		(0.021)	

Time-variant individual controls	Yes	Yes	Yes	Yes	Yes	Yes
Time-invariant individual controls	Yes	No	Yes	No	Yes	No
Individual FEs	No	Yes	No	Yes	No	Yes
Year FEs	Yes	Yes	Yes	Yes	Yes	Yes
Province FEs	Yes	Yes	Yes	Yes	Yes	Yes
Observations	2,597	2,583	2,597	2,583	2,597	2,583

Note: Growth rate is the moving average of normalized growth rate since assuming office. Time-invariant individual controls are *gender, college education, ethnicity* and time-variant individual controls are *age, position* (party secretary=1 and governor=0), *years in office* (a set of dummies indicating years two to twelve). Only coefficients of key independent variables are reported. FEs=fixed effects; GPSs=General Party Secretaries; PSC=Politburo Standing Committee.

*** p<0.01, ** p<0.05, * p<0.1. Robust standard errors clustered at the provincial level in parentheses.

often rooted in familial ties, marriages, shared birthplaces, and shared educational backgrounds, to consolidate their political control. In a system where peer and subordinate approvals are needed to stay in power, leaders naturally prioritize placing their allies in pivotal positions to ensure that their support network remains intact.

Four groups of researchers claim that they have found systematic evidence supporting the meritocratic argument based on prefecture and county-level data. However, various issues raise doubts about the validity of the findings in these publications. Wiebe (2024) combs through the dataset used by Chen and Kung (2019) and finds major coding errors in their key variables. After correction, economic growth can no longer predict prefecture leaders' promotion chances. Yao and Zhang (2015) report that economic performance improves prefecture leaders' promotion, but only for those above age fifty-one. This result, however, is not robust. Once two innocuous control variables are dropped, these findings disappear (Wiebe 2024). Zeng and Wong (2021) study both prefecture and county-level leaders and discover that higher GDP growth rate correlates with higher promotion rate. Their regression model is a simple cross-sectional analysis. In addition, it does not include patronage variables at all. It is too weak to support any solid conclusion. Compared with these studies, the paper by Landry, Lü, and Duan (2018) has better data quality and empirical design. While they do not confirm meritocratic promotion for prefecture leaders, they find a positive effect for county leaders. Wiebe (2024) is able to replicate this result even when model specifications are aligned with conventional approaches. From our earlier discussions, there are still two sources of problems with this result. First, their patronage variable utilizes formal appointment authority to identify an informal power relationship and inflates the patronage tie dramatically, as indicated earlier. Second, their model does not address the endogeneity problem in an adequate manner. Adding region and year fixed effects does not parse out the impact of individual specific traits that may have caused both high performance and a high probability of promotion. In sum, none of these published articles can provide a solid empirical foundation to support the meritocratic view at the prefecture and county levels.

At this stage, we do not have full datasets to directly test the meritocratic view with sub-provincial leaders. Researchers who adhere to the alternative definition of patronage ties require only the names of leaders, their official positions, and term information to establish these ties. For our measurement to work, we must go back to these leaders' official appointments preceding their current superior–inferior relationships. This approach involves gathering information on their positions, bureaucratic ranks, organization names, regional affiliations, and tenure durations. For sub-provincial officials, identifying names, positions, and terms over an extended period of time is already a formidable task, and compiling comprehensive biographies add further complexity. Oftentimes, lower-tier governments indicate only the name, gender, age, and party year on their websites but fail to disclose full information about their career paths. For earlier years, even the names of local leaders are hard to identify. However, constructing a long time series dataset remains crucial for the implementation of our empirical strategy and will be pursued in the coming years.

5 Patronage and Development Path: A New Research Agenda

We started this intellectual exploration with a central question in the realm of political economy: How do regime types impact a society's economic development outcomes? Specifically, does democracy hold any advantages in this regard? While earlier proponents of the democratic advantage argument highlighted the importance of structural and institutional elements, recent scholarship has attempted to establish the causal mechanism behind the superior personal qualities of democratically elected leaders. This intellectual pursuit has encountered significant challenges from scholars studying China's economic rise over the past four decades. According to these scholars, China's autocratic one-party state has implemented a system reminiscent of a tournament-competition structure to manage its officials. Leading officials across the country operate under contracts mandating the completion of quantified tasks assigned from higher authorities, particularly focusing on various economic indicators like GDP growth rate and fiscal revenue growth. Their performance is being routinely evaluated by superiors and is assigned with a merit rank within the cadre assessment system. Only leaders with outstanding merit ratings are considered for promotion. Consequently, this creates a meritocratic state where competence in economic development is rewarded, incentivizing high-quality leaders to rise to the top and govern the country. These scholars argue that China's successful economy challenges the claim that autocracies are inherently plagued by corruption and nepotism, presenting a compelling counterpoint to the notion of a democratic advantage.

Methodologically, grounding the challenge to the democratic advantage argument on the basis of a single case can be problematic. Observing the presence of a merit-based cadre evaluation system in tandem with China's thriving economy does not inherently substantiate a causal relationship. China's economic success is far more intricate than being a mere coincidence of a meritocratic cadre system, even if it exists in reality. Researchers have proposed many reasons underpinning China's economic growth, like agricultural liberalization, state-owned sector reforms, industrialization and urbanization drives, and increased participation in international trade (Naughton 2006; Su et al. 2012). These structural dimensions contribute significantly to China's growth story, casting doubts on overreliance on the meritocratic argument alone. Additionally, the finding that GDP growth boosts a leader's chance of promotion – an assertion found to be false according to our research – implies only that cadres may be incentivized to work harder for faster economic growth. But there has been no serious attempt to empirically verify this connection until a recent paper by Pang, Keng, and Zhang (2023). Unlike previous scholarship which studies if economic growth is rewarded with promotion, they directly test if the prospect of promotion can motivate local leaders to adopt pro-growth policies. They employ an innovative approach to assess leaders' initial likelihood in the promotion game and demonstrate that favored leaders have, in fact, not allocated more budgetary resources toward infrastructural spending or utilized financial vehicles to secure additional development funds. This directly contradicts the predictions hypothesized by the meritocratic view.

In this Element, we challenge the meritocratic perspective from a different angle and question its very existence within China's one-party system. Theoretically, this viewpoint does not offer a satisfying explanation for the emergence of a merit-based system in China. For power-conscious autocratic leaders, entrusting critical personnel decisions to an ostensibly objective system undermines their authority – a potentially fatal move in an autocracy. The absence of serious interrogation of power in this framework indicates an underappreciation of the inherent contradiction between competence and loyalty. Moreover, recent scholarship challenges the notion of a common existential threat uniting post-Mao elites behind a Weberian state. In factual terms, the meritocracy argument rests on misrepresentation of China's cadre assessment and promotion system. Contrary to claims of a quantitative scoring system favoring economic growth, cadres are evaluated across five categories – virtue (ideological correctness), ability, diligence, achievement, and integrity. While achievement may be measured by quantitative scores, final merit ratings are determined by subjective evaluations by peers, subordinates, and superiors, not from an objective scoring regimen. Furthermore, there is no inherent linkage between cadre performance and official promotions. The assessment system is really intended to coerce frontline cadres to carry out their official responsibilities. In practice, data manipulation also makes these evaluations practically useless for higher-level Departments of Organization. Upon addressing potential endogeneity issues, our empirical analysis demonstrates that provincial leaders with stronger GDP growth records do not consistently receive higher promotion chances, aligning with our theoretical critique discussed earlier.

We hope that our critical examination of the meritocratic view can prompt political economists to reevaluate the foundational assumptions of their approach, particularly concerning a merit-based system in China. While "growth for promotion" provides a concise mechanism for deriving testable hypotheses, its theoretical simplicity comes at the expense of misrepresenting reality and, more problematically, neglecting the crucial issue of power. Notably, an early proponent of the meritocratic argument has begun to acknowledge that cadre assessment results might not necessarily affect officials' chances of promotion or demotion (Zhou 2022). Instead of abandoning this approach, however, he proposes that the sense of honor or frustration generated as a result of the ranking system may be powerful enough to drive local leaders toward adopting pro-growth policies. This reformulation maintains the core claim of a merit-based system in China but has effectively grounded the causal mechanism from formal promotion to officials' psychological feelings, which is hard, if not impossible, to test empirically.

Our critical stance toward the meritocratic argument in explaining China's economic development post-Mao should not be interpreted as dismissing the value of studying the political foundation of economic growth. Echoing the sentiments expressed in the opening paragraph of this Element, we firmly support North's insight regarding the embedment of economic growth theories within a theory of the state. The type of regime can significantly shape not only the allocation of resources and policy decisions but also the overall trajectory of development. Moreover, regime types can play a pivotal role in determining the distribution of wealth within society, as well as the long-term sustainability of economic growth. The crucial point is to identify the appropriate causal mechanisms. Returning to the case discussed in this Element, if China's one-party autocracy has had any effect on its breakneck-fast growth in the past forty years, it cannot be a result of the high competence of its leaders. Some more promising areas for exploration can be found in the writings of political economists. For instance, in discussing the potential advantages of autocratic regimes, Bhagwati (2002) highlights its strength in mobilizing resources for investment, as well as the ability of ruling elites to be insulated from social pressure. Compared with other developing countries at a similar stage of development, an exceptionally high percentage of Chinese GDP goes toward investment (Su and Tao 2017). Governments at all levels have leveraged various forms of financial resources, such as state-owned enterprise profits, tax incomes, land lease fees, and loans both from banks and from financial platforms, for infrastructure construction across the country. In addition to state resources, the regime has utilized its coercive capacity to suppress dissenting voices from various social groups, such as workers, human rights activists, and regular citizens concerned about environmental pollution. The tranquility has fostered an extremely pro-business environment in China, prompting both domestic private businesses and international firms to invest heavily in industries, thus solidifying China's position as the world factory and enhancing the competitiveness of Chinese exports in the global market (Tao 2023).

The regime's ability of resource mobilization and social insulation is underpinning fast wealth creation in China. However, as cautioned by some scholars, the regime's traits also limit the potential for sustained development. Silenced groups are not benefiting equally from the economic boom in the way that the protected business class is, resulting in domestic demands falling short of supporting China's increasingly productive economy. Moreover, social insulation and repression mean that the regime is unable to fully utilize the vast talent within society and transition to an economy based on knowledge and technology, which are fundamental for long-term growth (Acemoglu and Robinson 2012). These analyses should enrich our understanding of the role of China's one-party system in its economy. Most important of all, similar analytical perspectives have been employed by researchers to explain the experiences of other developing countries, including Japan, South Korea, Taiwan, and Brazil. This approach could significantly facilitate comparative studies of diverse development experiences and foster the generation of new insights regarding the impact of regimes, while also encouraging the adoption of more rigorous and innovative empirical designs.

In addition to shedding light on the large debate about regime and development, future research could pursue another promising avenue of inquiry. Since our research concludes that patronage has been a central principle governing Chinese politics, it is only natural to ask how patronage politics has impacted China's economic development. Encouragingly, a few recent studies have ventured into this research direction, yielding fruitful outcomes. In the remaining section of this conclusion, we briefly introduce and discuss some representative pieces on this topic.

Zhang and Liu (2019) problematize the diverging economic trajectories within Zhejiang Province during the reform period. Even though Zhejiang is generally recognized as a leader in promoting private businesses, significant variations exist at sub-provincial levels. The authors attribute these disparities to the influence of patronage politics. Specifically, the pre-1949 revolution experience led to the emergence of two opposing elite factions: the southbound cadre group and the local guerrilla cadre group. Following the founding of the People's Republic of China, power struggles in the province marginalized the local guerrilla cadre group, causing it to lose powerful patrons in both the central government and the provincial government. Deprived of protection from vertical patron–client networks, these guerrilla cadres faced continual threats to their political survival, often becoming targets of political campaigns orchestrated by the southbound cadres. To survive, the local guerrilla cadres pursued a strategy of forging alliances with the local populations they governed. They shielded local entrepreneurs from hostile state policies and permitted extensive private economic activities. This de facto protection of property rights earned them grassroots political support, enhancing their chances of survival against political assaults from their rivals. Consequently, counties governed by local guerrilla cadres tended to exhibit stronger safeguards for private property rights and fostered more vibrant underground economy.

In contrast, southbound cadres enjoyed protection from influential patrons from higher echelons. Their primary agenda for political survival and advancement required them to comply with directives from these high-level patrons. As dominant political elites, the southbound cadres were motivated to uphold the socialist nature of the local economy and bolster their control over the state sector for continued access to jobs and benefits. When political tides moved in the leftist direction, they would eradicate private businesses to show allegiance to their patrons, irrespective of the detrimental effects on local economic interests. As a result, counties governed by these cadres often had weaker private sectors. These differences, solidified during the Cultural Revolution, grew more prominently when China started to embrace market reforms, leading to diverging development trajectories in Zhejiang Province. This power-centric explanation offers a refreshing perspective on the differing development paths during China's transition, contrasting the uniform pro-growth motivation under the meritocratic claim. Interestingly, Pang, Keng, and Zhong (2018) use all prefecture-level party secretaries' promotion data and discover a similar pattern of cadres falling into two categories of protégés and outsiders. Only protégés can be promoted with short tenures, beat the age clock, and rise to the top. On the other hand, most outsiders follow the strict tenure rule and ultimately face the hurdle of age limits. It will be interesting to see if the logic in Zhang and Liu (2019) can find support in this context.

Lei (2023) applies the same reasoning to explain the diverging development models observed across Chinese regions post the global financial crisis in 2008. In order to support the domestic economy battered by weak demands from the international market, the Chinese government initiated a 4 trillion yuan stimulus package aimed at bolstering growth. However, the allocation of these funds and programs was profoundly influenced by politics. Upon analyzing city-level statistics, the author discovers that political patronage has played a crucial role. In particular, cities whose top leaders had patronage ties with their provincial party secretaries in 2008–2009 made more public investment in infrastructure, surpassing the mean by 50 percent. Presumably, these regions received a larger share of stimulus program funds. Concurrently, this led to substantial borrowing by these municipal governments to complete the funded projects. On the other hand, cities lacking these patronage connections grappled with inadequate funds for infrastructure development and concentrated efforts on improving the business environment for private investors. In the short term, cities with patronage affiliations experienced faster growth in the industrial sector but not in the aggregate economy compared to their unaffiliated counterparts, albeit they were shouldering heavier public debt. Most importantly, the author contends that these diverging development strategies persisted post-stimulus, establishing themselves as entrenched paths. While the former continued to rely on public investment and accrue debts for growth, the latter leaned more toward fostering entrepreneurship and attracting private investment.

This Lei's article revises certain findings from an earlier paper in a similar vein. Jiang (2018) highlights a robust, positive impact of patronage ties on municipal economic growth rates. He asserts that these ties enable superiors to navigate information asymmetry and steer clients toward achieving the patrons' intended goals of fostering economic growth. Interestingly, Jiang notes that patronage ties do not necessarily bring additional resources to the connected cities. However, Lei (2023) proposes a contrary viewpoint by unveiling the redistributive effects of patronage. While Jiang (2018) contends that patronage generally benefits economic growth, Lei (2023) argues that it adversely affects economic performance overall, despite its potential for short-term growth spurts. Resolving these disparities warrants further empirical research. Given the long and ambiguous causal chain from patronage to aggregate economic growth, future investigations may benefit from conducting concrete analyses of specific economic factors and policy choices in between, as Lei (2023) has done in his paper. But these two authors do share a common ground in their definition of patronage ties. Both rely on the appointment of superiors during their tenure to define an inferior's patronage tie. However, as previously discussed, this definition has several flaws and needs more thoughtful consideration.

Zhang et al. (2023) delve into China's efforts to combat air pollution during the 2000s and dissect how patronage politics profoundly influenced the implementation of environmental regulations. Even though the central government reinforced environmental laws multiple times, the execution was significantly politicized. The authors employ satellite imagery to gauge particulate matter (PM2.5) pollution across Chinese cities and reveal a correlation: cities where party secretaries had patronage ties with provincial party secretaries exhibited higher PM2.5 levels compared to cities lacking such connections. Notably, this trend intensified post-2007 when the central government mandated environmental targets as part of one-vote-veto items on cadres' performance contract. Pre-2007, enforcement of environmental laws was uniformly inadequate across cities. However, with heightened stakes, city leaders leveraged their patronage networks to shield their polluting practices within their domains.

The study extends its investigation to firm-level pollution discharge data, confirming a similar pattern: firms operating in patronage-protected cities emitted higher levels of sulfur dioxide (SO_2) and waste gas into the air, along with increased chemical oxygen demand (COD) and wastewater into rivers. Remarkably, polluting firms did not channel extra profits into technological advancements or contribute substantially to municipal coffers through taxes. Instead, they raised expenditure on gifts, dining, travel, entertainment, and undisclosed expenses – presumably to secure protection from city leaders, government officials, and regulators. Their study also reveals broader consequences of patronage politics and showcases a deteriorated business environment in these regions. Following the activation of city party secretaries' patronage ties, the number of newly registered firms declined. These findings align with prior research indicating that patronage connections undermine local leaders' drive to safeguard property rights and foster an entrepreneurial, private economy (Lei 2023; Zhang and Liu 2019).

These studies represent only a subset of the comprehensive research adopting the patronage framework in many related academic fields. But they exemplify the potential of the patronage lens in unraveling the intricate tapestry of China's political economy. By placing power at the center of intellectual inquiry, the patronage framework offers more nuanced explanations for the adoption or rejection of certain economic and social policies, regardless of their abstract theoretical merits. This insight allows us not only to see China's staggering economic achievements but also to appreciate the many negative economic and social outcomes in the process. Finally, this patronage-based understanding of economic development is by no means limited to China. Scholars have applied this approach to explain British colonial administrators' investment and tax policies (Xu 2018), Brazilian student performance in public schools (Toral 2024), and local chiefs' ability to secure temporary classrooms in Zambia (Baldwin 2013). By embracing this analytical tool, Chinese scholars should be able to join other political economists and develop more sophisticated research agendas that advance our understanding of the connection between patronage and development.

References

Acemoglu, D., & Robinson, J. A. (2012). *Why Nations Fail: The Origins of Power, Prosperity, and Poverty*. New York: Crown Business.

Acemoglu, D., & Robinson, J. A. (2020). *The Narrow Corridor: States, Societies, and the Fate of Liberty*. Penguin.

Acemoglu, D., Egorov, G., & Sonin, K. (2012). Dynamics and stability of constitutions, coalitions, and clubs. *American Economic Review*, 102(4), pp. 1446–1476.

Alesina, A., Baqir, R., & Easterly, W. (1999). Public goods and ethnic divisions. *Quarterly Journal of Economics*, 114(4), pp. 1243–1284.

An, H., Chen, Y., Luo, D., & Zhang, T. (2016). Political uncertainty and corporate investment: Evidence from China. *Journal of Corporate Finance*, 36, pp. 174–189.

Baldwin, K. (2013). Why vote with the chief? Political connections and public goods provision in Zambia. *American Journal of Political Science*, 57(4), pp. 794–809.

Bell, D. A. (2016). *The China Model*. Princeton University Press.

Besley, T., & Case, A. (1992). Incumbent behavior: Vote seeking, tax setting and yardstick competition. NBER working paper, 4041.

Besley, T., & Reynal-Querol, M. (2011). Do democracies select more educated leaders? *American Political Science Review*, 105(3), pp. 552–566.

Besley, T. J., Burgess, R., Khan, A., & Xu, G. (2021). Bureaucracy and development. NBER working paper, 29163.

Besley, T., Montalvo, J. G., & Reynal-Querol, M. (2011). Do educated leaders matter? *Economic Journal*, 121(554), pp. 205–227.

Bhagwati, J. N. (2002). Democracy and development: Cruel dilemma or symbiotic relationship? *Review of Development Economics*, 6(2), pp. 151–162.

Blanchard, O., & Shleifer, A. (2001). Federalism with and without political centralization: China versus Russia. *IMF Staff Papers*, 48(1), pp. 171–179.

Bo, Z. (1996). Economic performance and political mobility: Chinese provincial leaders. *Journal of Contemporary China*, 5(12), pp. 135–154.

Boix, C., & Svolik, M. W. (2013). The foundations of limited authoritarian government: Institutions, commitment, and power-sharing in dictatorships. *Journal of Politics*, 75(2), pp. 300–316.

Brandt, L., & Rawski, T. G. (2020). China's great boom as a historical process. IZA discussion paper, 13940.

Buckley, N., & Reuter, O. J. (2019). Performance incentives under autocracy: Evidence from Russia's regions. *Comparative Politics*, 51(2), pp. 239–266.

Central Committee of the CCP. (1986). *Notice from the Central Committee of the Communist Party of China on Strictly Selecting and Appointing Cadres in Accordance with Party Principles*. Available at: http://cpc.people.com.cn/BIG5/64162/71380/71387/71591/4855033.html.

Central Committee of the CCP. (1995). *Interim Provisions on the Selection and Appointment of Party and Government Leading Cadres*. Available at: www.gov.cn/gongbao/shuju/1995/gwyb199512.pdf.

Central Committee of the CCP. (2002). *Regulations on the Selection and Appointment of Party and Government Leading Cadres*. Available at: www.itp.cas.cn/djykxwh/llxx/dnfg/202011/t20201124_5777779.html.

Central Committee of the CCP. (2014). *Regulations on the Selection and Appointment of Party and Government Leading Cadres*. Available at: www.gov.cn/govweb/jrzg/2014-01/15/content_2567800.htm.

Central Committee of the CCP. (2019). *Regulations on the Selection and Appointment of Party and Government Leading Cadres*. Available at: www.gov.cn/zhengce/2019-03/17/content_5374532.htm.

Central Department of Organization. (1979). *Opinions on Implementing a Cadre Assessment System*. Available at: http://cpc.people.com.cn/BIG5/64162/71380/71387/71591/4854973.html.

Central Department of Organization. (1988). *Annual Work Assessment Scheme (Trial) for County (City, District) Party and Government Leading Cadres*. Available at: www.elinklaw.com/zsglmobile/lawView.aspx?id=30168.

Central Department of Organization. (1998). *Interim Provisions on the Assessment of Party and Government Leading Cadres*. Available at: http://cpc.people.com.cn/BIG5/64162/71380/71382/71480/4853966.html.

Central Department of Organization. (2006). *Comprehensive Assessment and Evaluation Measures for Local Party and Government Leadership Teams and Cadres in Accordance with the Requirements of the Scientific Development Concept*. Available at: https://zzb.nju.edu.cn/48/76/c1324a18550/pagem.htm.

Central Department of Organization. (2009a). *Annual Assessment Method for Party and Government Leadership Teams and Cadres (Trial)*. Available at: https://baike.sogou.com/v85311042.htm.

Central Department of Organization. (2009b). *Local Party and Government Leadership Team and Cadre Comprehensive Assessment and Evaluation Method (Trial)*. Available at: www.xbhao.net/zixun/4752.html.

Central Department of Organization. (2019). A press release on the *Regulations on the Assessment of Party and Government Leading Cadres*. Available at: www.gov.cn/zhengce/2019-04/22/content_5384987.htm.

Central Department of Organization Party Building Institute (2014). *Some Cadres Violated Rules and Promoted Secretaries to Leave Backdoors Open.* Available at: http://news.sina.com.cn/c/2014-07-06/044330475364 .shtml.

Chen, Y., Li, H., & Zhou, L. A. (2005). Relative performance evaluation and the turnover of provincial leaders in China. *Economics Letters,* 88(3), pp. 421–425.

Chen, S., Qiao, X., & Zhu, Z. (2021). Chasing or cheating? Theory and evidence on China's GDP manipulation. *Journal of Economic Behavior and Organization,* 189, pp. 657–671.

Chen, T., & Kung, J. S. (2016). Do land revenue windfalls create a political resource curse? Evidence from China. *Journal of Development Economics,* 123, pp. 86–106.

Chen, T., & Kung, J. K. S. (2019). Busting the "Princelings": The campaign against corruption in China's primary land market. *Quarterly Journal of Economics,* 134(1), pp. 185–226.

Choi, E. K. (2012). Patronage and performance: Factors in the political mobility of provincial leaders in post-Deng China. *China Quarterly,* 212, pp. 965–981.

Choi, E. K., Givens, J. W., & MacDonald, A. (2021). From power balance to dominant faction in Xi Jinping's China. *China Quarterly,* 248(1), pp. 935–956.

Cooter, R. (2003). Who gets on top in democracy? Elections as filters. *Supreme Court Economic Review,* 10, pp. 127–141.

Cruz, C., Labonne, J., & Querubin, P. (2017). Politician family networks and electoral outcomes: Evidence from the Philippines. *American Economic Review,* 107(10), pp. 3006–3037.

Dal Bó, E., Finan, F., Folke, O., Persson, T., & Rickne, J. (2017). Who becomes a politician? *Quarterly Journal of Economics,* 132(4), pp. 1877–1914.

De Mesquita, B. B., & Smith, A. (2011). *The Dictator's Handbook: Why Bad Behavior Is Almost Always Good Politics.* Public Affairs.

De Mesquita, B. B., Smith, A., Siverson, R. M., & Morrow, J. D. (2005). *The Logic of Political Survival.* MIT Press.

Deng, X. (1978). Liberate the mind, seek truth from facts, unite and look forward. In *Selected Works of Deng Xiaoping,* vol. 2. Beijing: People's Press.

Dittmer, L. (1995). Chinese informal politics. *China Journal,* 34, pp. 1–34.

Egorov, G., & Sonin, K. (2011). Dictators and their viziers: Endogenizing the loyalty–competence trade-off. *Journal of the European Economic Association,* 9(5), pp. 903–930.

Eisenman, J. (2018). *China's Green Revolution.* Columbia University Press.

Feng, J. (2010). Cadres in Zhong County [Zhongxian Ganbu]. PhD dissertation, Peking University. Available at: https://shorturl.at/Vp6i9.

Ferguson, J., & Kim, O. (2023). *Reassessing China's Rural Reforms: The View from Outer Space*. Mimeo. Berkeley: University of California Press.

Fewsmith, J. (2021). *Rethinking Chinese Politics*. Cambridge University Press.

Fisman, R., Shi, J., Wang, Y., & Wu, W. (2020). Social ties and the selection of China's political elite. *American Economic Review*, 110(6), pp. 1752–1781.

Francois, P., Trebbi, F., & Xiao, K. (2023). Factions in nondemocracies: Theory and evidence from the Chinese Communist Party. *Econometrica*, 91(2), pp. 565–603.

Gansu Provincial Department of Organization. (2023). *Use Assessments as a Guide and Promote a Competitive Environment for Achievements*. Available at: www.gszg.gov.cn/2023-04/11/c_1129511412.htm.

General Office of the Central Committee of the CCP. (2019). *Regulations on the Assessment of Party and Government Leading Cadres*. Available at: www .gov.cn/zhengce/2019-04/21/content_5384955.htm.

Gong, L., Xiao, J., & Zhang, Q. (2017). Promotion incentive: Corruption and its implications on local fiscal cycles in China. *Procedia Engineering*, 198, pp. 845–893.

Guo, X. (2001). Dimensions of guanxi in Chinese elite politics. *China Journal*, 46, pp. 69–90.

Huang, J. (1994). *Factionalism in Chinese Communist Politics*. Harvard University Press.

Huang, R. (2022). *Provincialism: Before Ruling China, You Have to Rule 2.4 Provinces*. Available at: https://macropolo.org/provincialism-ruling-china-provinces/?rp=m.

Jia, R., Kudamatsu, M., & Seim, D. (2015). Political selection in China: The complementary roles of connections and performance. *Journal of the European Economic Association*, 13(4), pp. 631–668.

Jiang, J. (2018). Making bureaucracy work: Patronage networks, performance incentives, and economic development in China. *American Journal of Political Science*, 62(4), pp. 982–999.

Jiang, J., & Luo, Z. (2021). Leadership styles and political survival of Chinese Communist Party elites. *Journal of Politics*, 83(2), pp. 777–782.

Jones, B. F., & Olken, B. A. (2005). Do leaders matter? National leadership and growth since World War II. *Quarterly Journal of Economics*, 120(3), pp. 835–864.

Keller, F. B. (2016). Moving beyond factions: Using social network analysis to uncover patronage networks among Chinese elites. *Journal of East Asian Studies*, 16(1), pp. 17–41.

Kou, C.-W. (2007). CYL cadres rising in the era of Hu Jintao: Factional considerations or organizational mission of channeling cadres. *Prospect Journal*, 3, pp. 77–116.

Kou, C.-W. (2014). The rise of youth league affiliates and their paths to the top. In Kou, C.-W., & Zang, X. (Eds.). *Choosing China's Leaders*. Routledge, pp. 142–164.

Landé, C. H. (1973). Networks and groups in Southeast Asia: Some observations on the group theory of politics. *American Political Science Review*, 67(1), pp. 103–127.

Landry, P. F., Lü, X., & Duan, H. (2018). Does performance matter? Evaluating political selection along the Chinese administrative ladder. *Comparative Political Studies*, 51(8), pp. 1074–1105.

Lazarsfeld, P. F., & Merton, R. K. (1954). Friendship as a social process: A substantive and methodological analysis. *Freedom and Control in Modern Society*, 18(1), pp. 18–66.

Lee, H. Y. (1991). *From Revolutionary Cadres to Party Technocrats in Socialist China*. University of California Press.

Lei, Z. (2023). The political resource blessing or curse? Patronage networks, infrastructure investment, and economic development in China. *Comparative Political Studies*, 56(8), pp. 1156–1188.

Li, H., & Zhou, L.-A. (2005). Political turnover and economic performance: The incentive role of personnel control in China. *Journal of Public Economics*, 89 (9–10), pp. 1743–1762.

Liu, B., Huang, K., & Wang, L. (2018). Who is more willing to reduce inventory: State-owned or non-state-owned real estate enterprises? *Economics Research*, 6, pp. 112–126.

Manion, M. (2023). *Political Selection in China: Rethinking Foundations and Findings*. Cambridge University Press.

Maskin, E., Qian, Y., & Xu, C. (2000). Incentives, information, and organizational form. *Review of Economic Studies*, 67(2), pp. 359–378.

Mattingly, D. C. (2024). How the party commands the gun: The foreign–domestic threat dilemma in China. *American Journal of Political Science*, 68(1), pp. 227–242.

Mei, D., Wang, Z., & Lei, W. (2014). The opening of the party congress, changes in supervision intensity, and economic fluctuations in China. *Economics Research*, 3, pp. 47–61.

Moore, B. (1993 [1966]). *Social Origins of Dictatorship and Democracy: Lord and Peasant in the Making of the Modern World* (No. 268). Boston, MA: Beacon Press.

Nathan, A. (1973). A factionalism model for CCP politics. *China Quarterly*, 53, pp. 34–66.

Naughton, B. J. (2006). *The Chinese Economy: Transitions and Growth*. MIT Press.

North, D. C. (1981). *Structure and Change in Economic History*. Norton.

North, D. C., & Weingast, B. R. (1989). Constitutions and commitment: The evolution of institutions governing public choice in seventeenth-century England. *Journal of Economic History*, 49(4), pp. 803–832.

Oi, J. (1999). *Rural China Takes Off: Institutional Foundations of Economic Reform*. University of California Press.

Opper, S., Nee, V., & Brehm, S. (2015). Homophily in the career mobility of China's political elite. *Social Science Research*, 54, pp. 332–352.

Pang, B., Keng, S., & Zhang, S. (2023) Does performance competition impact China's leadership behavior? Re-examining the promotion tournament hypothesis. *China Quarterly*, 255, pp. 716–733.

Pang, B. Keng, S., & Zhong, L. (2018) Sprinting with small steps: China's cadre management and authoritarian resilience. *China Journal*, 80, pp. 68–93.

People's Daily. (2019). Strictly control "one-vote-veto" items to reduce burdens for grassroots government and to support real work. March 28.

Przeworski, A., & Limongi, F. (1993). Political regimes and economic growth. *Journal of Economic Perspectives*, 7(3), pp. 51–69.

Qian, Y., & Xu, C. (1993). The M-form hierarchy and China's economic reform. *European Economic Review*, 37(2–3), pp. 541–548.

Sheng, Y. (2022). Performance-based authoritarianism revisited: GDP growth and the political fortunes of China's provincial leaders. *Modern China*, 48(5), pp. 982–1018.

Shih, V. C. (2008). *Factions and Finance in China: Elite Conflict and Inflation*. Cambridge University Press.

Shih, V., Adolph. C., & Liu, M. (2012). Getting ahead in the communist party: Explaining the advancement of central committee members in China. *American Political Science Review*, 106(1), pp. 166–187.

Su, F., Tao, R., Xi, L., & Li, M. (2012). Local officials' incentives and China's economic growth: Tournament thesis reexamined and alternative explanatory framework. *China and World Economy*, 20(4), pp. 1–18.

Su, F., & Tao, R. (2017). The China model withering? Institutional roots of China's local developmentalism. *Urban Studies*, 54(1), pp. 230–250.

Svolik, M. (2012). *The Politics of Authoritarian Rule*. Cambridge University Press.

Tao, R. (2023). The formation, evolution and regulation of China's growth model. *Twenty-First Century Review*, 195, pp. 4–28.

Tao, R., Su, F., Xi, L., & Zhu, Y. (2010). Can economic growth increase promotion? A logic challenge to the tournament thesis and an empirical reassessment. *Management World*, 12, pp. 13–26.

Tao, Y., Liu, M., & Hou, L. (2020). *Local Governance Practice: Structure and Effect*. Social Science Literature Press.

Toral, G. (2024). How patronage delivers: Political appointments, bureaucratic accountability, and service delivery in Brazil. *American Journal of Political Science*, 68(2), pp. 797–815.

Tsai, P.-H. (2016). Fiscal incentives and political budget cycles in China. *International Tax and Public Finance*, 23, pp. 1030–1073.

Wallace, J. L. (2016). Juking the stats? Authoritarian information problems in China. *British Journal of Political Science*, 46(1), pp. 11–29.

Wang, Z., Zhang, Q., & Zhou, L.-A. (2020). Career incentives of city leaders and urban spatial expansion in China. *Review of Economics and Statistics*, 102(5), pp. 897–911.

Whiting, S. (2006). *Power and Wealth in Rural China: The Political Economy of Institutional Change*. Cambridge University Press.

Wiebe, M. (2024). Replicating the literature on prefecture-level meritocratic promotion in China. *Research and Politics*, 11(1). https://doi.org/10.1177/20531680241229875.

Wooldridge, J. M. (2010). *Econometric Analysis of Cross Section and Panel Data*. Cambridge, MA: MIT Press.

Xi, Jinping. (2014). *A Speech at the Fourth Plenary Meeting of 18th Party Congress*. Available at: https://m.ccdi.gov.cn/content/40/f5/15481.html.

Xu, C. (2011). The fundamental institutions of China's reforms and development. *Journal of Economic Literature*, 49(4), pp. 1076–1151.

Xu, G. (2018). The costs of patronage: Evidence from the British empire. *American Economic Review*, 108(11), pp. 3170–3198.

Xu, Y., Qian, X., & Li, W. (2013). Political uncertainty, political connections and private firm investment: Evidence from city party secretaries. *Management World*, 5, pp. 116–130.

Yan, H. (2017). *In and Out of Central Department of Organization: Another Life of a Red Idealist*. Hong Kong: Mingjing Press.

Yao, Y., & Zhang, M. (2015). Subnational leaders and economic growth: Evidence from Chinese cities. *Journal of Economic Growth*, 20, pp. 405–436.

Zeng, Y., & Wong, S. H. W. (2021). Time is power: Rethinking meritocratic political selection in China. *China Quarterly*, 245, pp. 23–50.

Zhang, C., Tao, R., Su, F., & Li, M. (2023). Political protection, pollution control, and economic consequences: Evidence from China's battle over the clean air. Working paper.

Zhang, Q., & Liu, M. (2019). *Revolutionary Legacy, Power Structure, and Grassroots Capitalism under the Red Flag in China.* Cambridge University Press.

Zhou, L.-A. (2022). Promotion tournament: Literature review and future research. *Quarterly Journal of Economics and Management* (Chinese), 1(1), pp. 1–34.

Zhu, Y., & Xu, D. (2013). Officials' promotion pressure, financial market and housing price increase. *Finance Research*, 1, pp. 65–78.

Zhu, P., & Ye, F. (2013). Establishing a cadre assessment mechanism that promotes scientific development: A summary of experts' and scholars' research. *People's Daily*, July 30. Available at: http://theory.people.com.cn/n/2013/0730/c367180-22382839.html.

Cambridge Elements ☰

Chinese Economy and Governance

Luke Qi Zhang
Fudan University

Luke Qi Zhang is Associate Professor at the China Center for Economic Studies of the School of Economics at Fudan University. He specializes in the political economy of authoritarianism generally and how elite politics affects policy making and economic outcomes in China specifically. His book (co-authored with Mingxing Liu) *Revolutionary Legacy, Power Structure, and Grassroots Capitalism under the Red Flag in China* (Cambridge University Press, 2019) proposes a theory of localized property rights protection under authoritarianism, and applies the theory to the private sector development in both the Mao era and the current reform era in China.

Mingxing Liu
Peking University

Mingxing Liu is Professor of the China Institute for Educational Finance Research at Peking University. He works on China's elite politics, economic growth, and local governance. He has published numerous academic articles in international and Chinese journals such as the *American Political Science Review, Comparative Political Studies, Comparative Politics,* and *Journal of Politics.*

Daniel Mattingly
Yale University

Daniel Mattingly is Associate Professor in the Department of Political Science at Yale University. He studies the domestic and international politics of authoritarian regimes, with a focus on China. His book *The Art of Political Control in China* (Cambridge University Press, 2020) received the Best Book Award from the Democracy and Autocracy Section of the American Political Science Association and was named a best book of the year by *Foreign Affairs.*

About the Series

The works in this Elements series examine China's economy, governance, and policy-making process. Members of the political and business communities will find the series a valuable guide to navigate China's complex policy and governance system and understand its business environment.

Cambridge Elements ≡

Chinese Economy and Governance

Elements in the Series

Meritocracy or Patronage? Political Foundations of China's Economic Transition
Fubing Su and Ran Tao

A full series listing is available at: www.cambridge.org/ECEG

Printed in the United States
by Baker & Taylor Publisher Services